21.20   REF

THE FOUNDING OF AMERICA

**GREAT
SPEECHES
IN
HISTORY**

Leora Maltz, *Book Editor*

Daniel Leone, *President*

Bonnie Szumski, *Publisher*

Scott Barbour, *Managing Editor*

Greenhaven Press, Inc.
San Diego, California

Library of Congress Cataloging-in-
Publication Data

The founding of America / Leora Maltz,
book editor.
    p. cm. — (The Greenhaven Press great
speeches in history)
    Includes bibliographical references and
index.
    ISBN 0-7377-0870-0 (pbk. : alk. paper) —
    ISBN 0-7377-0871-9 (lib. : alk. paper)
    1. United States—Politics and government—To
1775—Sources. 2. United States—Politics and
government—1775–1783—Sources. 3. United
States—Politics and government—1783–
1865—Sources. 4. Liberty—Political aspects—
United States—History—Sources. 5. Freedom
of speech—United States—History—Sources.
6. Speeches, addresses, etc., American. I. Maltz,
Leora. II. Series.

E187 .F73 2002
973.3—dc21   2001040736
                                          CIP

© 2002 by Greenhaven Press, Inc.
10911 Technology Place
San Diego, CA 92127

Printed in the U.S.A.

Contents

issued a mere month before the battles of Concord and Lexington.

Chapter 2: Fundamental Principles of Democracy: Liberty and Free Speech

Chapter 3: Debating the Constitution

Chapter 4: The Native American Speaks

Foreword

I have a dream that one day this nation will rise up and live out the true meaning of its creed: "We hold these truths to be self-evident: that all men are created equal."

I have a dream that one day on the red hills of Georgia the sons of former slaves and the sons of former slave owners will be able to sit down together at the table of brotherhood.

I have a dream that one day even the state of Mississippi, a state sweltering with the heat of injustice, sweltering with the heat of oppression, will be transformed into an oasis of freedom and justice.

I have a dream that my four little children will one day live in a nation where they will not be judged by the color of their skin but by the content of their character.

Perhaps no speech in American history resonates as deeply as Martin Luther King Jr.'s "I Have a Dream," delivered in 1963 before a rapt audience of 250,000 on the steps of the Lincoln Memorial in Washington, D.C. Decades later, the speech still enthralls those who read or hear it, and stands as a philosophical guidepost for contemporary discourse on racism.

What distinguishes "I Have a Dream" from the hundreds of other speeches given during the civil rights era are King's eloquence, lyricism, and use of vivid metaphors to convey abstract ideas. Moreover, "I Have a Dream" serves not only as a record of history—a testimony to the racism that permeated American society during the 1960s—but it is also a historical event in its own right. King's speech, aired live on national television, marked the first time that the grave injustice of racism was fully articulated to a mass audience in a way that was both logical and evocative. Julian Bond, a fellow participant in the civil rights movement and student of King's, states that

> King's dramatic 1963 "I Have a Dream" speech before the Lincoln Memorial cemented his place as first among equals in civil rights leadership; from this first televised mass meeting, an American audience saw and heard the unedited oratory of America's finest preacher, and for the first time, a mass white audience heard the undeniable justice of black demands.

Moreover, by helping people to understand the justice of the civil rights movement's demands, King's speech helped to transform the nation. In 1964, a year after the speech was delivered, President Lyndon B. Johnson signed the Civil Rights Act, which outlawed segregation in public facilities and discrimination in employment. In 1965, Congress passed the Voting Rights Act, which forbids restrictions, such as literacy tests, that were commonly used in the South to prevent blacks from voting. King's impact on the country's laws illustrates the power of speech to bring about real change.

Greenhaven Press's Great Speeches in History series offers students an opportunity to read and study some of the greatest speeches ever delivered before an audience. Each volume traces a specific historical era, event, or theme through speeches—both famous and lesser known. An introductory essay sets the stage by presenting background and context. Then a collection of speeches follows, grouped in chapters based on chronology or theme. Each selection is preceded by a brief introduction that offers historical context, biographical information about the speaker, and analysis of the speech. A comprehensive index and an annotated table of contents help readers quickly locate material of interest, and a bibliography serves as a launching point for further research. Finally, an appendix of author biographies provides detailed background on each speaker's life and work. Taken together, the volumes in the Greenhaven Great Speeches in History series offer students vibrant illustrations of history and demonstrate the potency of the spoken word. By reading speeches in their historical context, students will be transported back in time and gain a deeper understanding of the issues that confronted people of the past.

Introduction

Historians often pinpoint the 1763 Treaty of Paris, which ended the Anglo-French wars, as a pivotal date in the development of American independence. For several decades prior to this point, the Americans and the British had been involved in repeated skirmishes with the French. However, in 1756 these hostilities escalated into a full-blown war that lasted until 1763 and became known as the Seven Years' War. During these years, Britain and France fought each other for control of North America's western border, with its river access and its profitable fur trade. France, which had successfully controlled the region for nearly a hundred years, initially dominated the war, but ultimately Britain succeeded in capturing the strategic forts on the western front and thereby gained control of the region. In winning the war, the British (with the help of many American recruits) successfully destroyed French hopes of a North American empire. Under the 1763 Treaty of Paris, France had to relinquish its American territories and turn over Florida to its Spanish allies.

Besides thwarting France's colonial aspirations, the war had other consequences that ultimately contributed to American independence. It not only united American troops from various parts of the country, but it also gave them the opportunity to prove themselves militarily successful. Often, American generals such as George Washington strategized campaigns for the local terrain far more astutely than their British counterparts, and Americans began to gain confidence in their military prowess. Furthermore, the peace treaty of 1763 removed the immediate threat of the French.

Thus, lacking their longtime enemies, the American colonists no longer needed British protection and gradually began to perceive Britain not as a guardian but instead as a foreign power with increasingly disparate interests. Finally, the Seven Years' War with France had emptied the coffers of the British Crown. Britain's attempts to raise taxes from the Americans in order to help finance the war were the impetus for the initial political sparring between the American colonists and their mother country. The conclusion of the war thus ushered in a new era in which the British government both increased taxes in America and tightened its control over the regional governments set up in the American colonies.

Excessive Taxation

By 1764, a year after the Treaty of Paris formally ended the war, British treasury minister Lord George Grenville had already begun to incite colonial fury by introducing the Sugar Act. Heavily taxing molasses imported from non-British countries while tightening customs controls, the Sugar Act provoked the first of a series of boycotts of British manufactured goods. Matters only worsened in the following year, when Grenville succeeded in outraging even more Americans with the Stamp Act, which mandated that stamps be bought and placed on all newspapers, commercial and legal documents, and even playing cards. The acts prompted massive protests and sparked debates about the legality of "taxation without representation": The colonists were being directly taxed by Britain, yet they lacked representation in the British Parliament. Meanwhile, the astute propagandist Samuel Adams organized grassroots resistance and was instrumental in the founding of the Sons of Liberty—groups of American men organized into regional chapters to oppose the Stamp Act. They did this by preventing the sale of stamps, which were legally demanded for countless daily commercial transactions, thereby ensuring that business continued as usual without the mandatory stamps. The Sons of Liberty were also responsible for the boycott of British goods and for the non-payment of British merchants whose goods had already been brought. Invasive British laws, and raised taxes, thus initiated the organization and resistance of the American colonists.

In the southern colony of Virginia, the young statesman Patrick Henry responded to the Stamp Act in a different way: He penned a letter condemning the British tax. Henry's letter was widely published throughout the colonies and served to publicize the widespread public outrage at Britain. In October 1765 a group of state leaders, including Henry and the more moderate John Dickinson of Pennsylvania, met at the Stamp Act Congress to resolve the taxation crisis in unison, overcoming their political differences in their common anger at British policies. The document that emerged from their meeting was a petition that was sent to the British king and the two houses of Parliament in which both the "rights and the grievances of the colonists of America" were expressed. Yet the tone of the statement was mild, and Dickinson, who effectively drafted much of the document, stressed continued American loyalty to the Crown.

The British Parliament, in recognition of the colonists' protests and in response to the complaints by British merchants who were losing large sums of money by the American boycott of British goods, were leaning toward revoking the Stamp Tax. However, the British Crown did not want to be embarrassed by appearing to bow to the demands of a colony. A face-saving solution to the dilemma was found: Benjamin Franklin, who was residing in London at the time as the colonial agent, was asked to represent the Americans and testify on the subject of the Stamp Tax. Franklin argued that the Americans did not take issue with what he called "external" taxes (taxes on goods *before* they were brought into America), but rather that they objected strongly to "internal" taxes (those levied at a local level). In fact, many historians have argued that this distinction was more semantic than real and that few Americans had actually made such a differentiation. It nonetheless clothed the American complaints in a certain logic, thus enabling the British Parliament to rescind the Stamp Tax in 1766 while leaving the door open to enact future "external" taxes.

Yet as they removed the Stamp Tax, the British buttressed their position by announcing the 1766 Declaratory Act, which clarified Britain's absolute right "to bind the colonies in all cases whatsoever." Thus reiterating the power of the British Crown, this statement of authority portended future conflicts, for the Stamp Act crisis was barely over when the notorious Townshend Acts of 1767 were announced, taxing a whole new array of imported British goods (including lead, glass, tea, and paper). These taxes were external taxes levied primarily on luxury goods, so the British hoped that they would not incite excessive opposition. However, the Americans viewed this tactic as a thinly disguised ploy to continue to drain their funds, and they were widely resentful. By now the American colonists were adept at economic resistance, and they quickly reorganized their protest efforts to boycott British merchandise. As the largest buyer of British goods, the North Americans succeeded once again in quickly and dramatically reducing British export revenues. One of the most famous responses to the Townshend Taxes came in the form of a series of letters penned by John Dickinson entitled "Letters from a Farmer in Pennsylvania to the Inhabitants of the British Colonies." In this publication, which was the most widely read essay by an American during the colonial period, Dickinson argued that the Townshend Taxes were unconstitutional because their purpose was not to regulate trade but explicitly to raise revenue.

Excessive British taxes had made customs officials, the enforcers of these tariffs, extremely unpopular figures in the port cities of Boston, Providence, and New York. They not only became targets to be lampooned in the media, but they were also occasionally attacked. In a famous incident in June 1768, the wealthiest Boston merchant and renowned patriot, John Hancock, had his ship *Liberty* seized by customs officials on the suspicion that it was carrying smuggled goods (which it was). A crowd gathered at the docks, and a riot ensued. The British customs officials were forced to flee for their lives, and their property was destroyed. In an angry response to this hounding of British officials, the British government sent troops into Boston. Two regiments arrived later in 1768, filling Boston with British redcoats and irrevocably raising tensions in the Massachusetts capital.

In April 1770 a new British prime minister, Lord Frederick North, took over and persuaded the British Parliament to

repeal the unpopular Townshend Acts. However, this concession was not enough to dissipate the mounting anger at
British tax policies and political absolutism. Tensions in
Boston ran high, with matters coming to a head in March
1770 when a group of rioting Bostonians pelted British
guards with stones encased in snowballs. According to reports, one guard fell over, and suddenly confusion reigned as
the soldiers opened fire on their attackers, shooting and
killing five men. The incident was soon being referred to by
Americans as the Boston Massacre, but the guards, who acted
against orders, claimed at their trial to have been scared and
outnumbered. Defended by the American patriots John
Adams and Josiah Quincy, the Boston jury acquitted the
British soldiers. In time the soldiers were soon forgotten, but
the five Bostonians became martyrs who were commemorated
annually as heroes in the struggle for American liberty.

The massacre spotlighted Boston as the central stage in
the unfolding political drama, and the city continued to be
the epicenter of political tension for the next few years. It
was during this charged atmosphere that the British Parliament passed the Tea Act, mandating that Americans must
buy British tea exclusively. The Tea Act had been passed in
order to resuscitate the flailing fortunes of the East India
Company, whose London warehouse was overflowing with
17 million pounds of unsold tea, driving down stock values
and forcing the company into near bankruptcy. Parliament
decided to unload the excess tea on American consumers by
radically dropping the price of British tea until it cost the
same as the inferior Dutch tea that Americans typically
drank. But by this point the colonists were so suspicious of
the British government's efforts to control their imports that
they refused to buy the British tea, arguing that it prevented
them from trading freely on the international market. At the
famous Boston Tea Party in December 1773, Samuel Adams
led a group of men dressed as Indians onto the cargo ships,
where they ceremoniously emptied precious cargoes of
British tea into Boston's harbor. Subsequent "tea parties" in
New York, New Jersey, and Maryland similarly destroyed
other shiploads of tea in defiance of British authority.

After the Boston Tea Party, events leading to the Ameri-

can Revolution quickly snowballed. The British imposed a
series of Coercive Acts against Boston, revoking the Massachusetts charter and closing the harbor. Town meetings were
restricted, the right to trial by public juries was revoked, and
the capital was moved to Salem, Massachusetts. British gen-

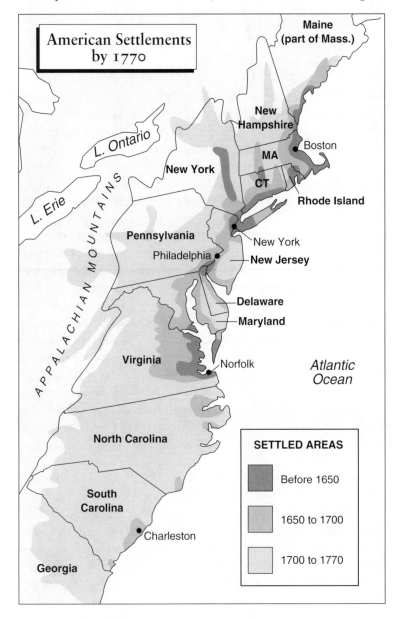

American Settlements
by 1770

Maine
(part of Mass.)

New
Hampshire

L. Ontario

New York

MA

Boston

L. Erie

APPALACHIAN MOUNTAINS

CT

Rhode Island

Pennsylvania

New York

Philadelphia

New Jersey

Delaware

Maryland

Virginia

Norfolk

Atlantic
Ocean

North Carolina

South
Carolina

Charleston

Georgia

SETTLED AREAS

Before 1650

1650 to 1700

1700 to 1770

eral Thomas Gage was sent to Boston with the dual title of commander in chief of the British armed forces and governor of Massachusetts. People all over the country rallied to support the Bostonians during this difficult time, sending donations of money, and within days of Gage's arrival calls were being made for a meeting between the colonies in order to implement a unified response to the Coercive Acts.

The First Continental Congress

This meeting came to be known as the First Continental Congress and was held in Philadelphia in September 1774, with every colony except Georgia sending a representative. Although most American colonists at this time still perceived themselves to be loyal to the British king and had no express desire to sever that bond, there was, nonetheless, widespread condemnation of Parliament, and the delegates had much to complain about. In addition to coordinating a plan of resistance against the British government, the delegates also endeavored to precisely articulate their grievances: The result was a document entitled the "Declaration of Rights and Grievances." In it, there was no mention of independence but rather a request for restraint and fairness and specifically for the repeal of the Coercive Acts and other objectionable taxes. Underlying the Americans' cooperative tone was the assumption that they would continue to oppose future taxes to raise revenues. Meanwhile, an economic boycott of all English and Irish goods was being put into effect, and American goods were no longer being exported to Britain. Importantly, it was also decided at the First Continental Congress that a militia needed to be raised and armed. Toward the end of the congress, in October 1774, Patrick Henry made his famous statement in which he attempted to elevate national identity over state identity, saying, "The distinctions between New Englanders and Virginians are no more. I am no longer a Virginian but an American." Although most of the colonists still viewed themselves foremost as members of their state or their town, Henry's comment became famous for marking the beginning of the formation of a national consciousness as an American people.

Before leaving, the delegates to the First Continental Congress decided to meet again the following May. However, before that second meeting was to occur, the first gunfire of the war had already been exchanged in the battles at Lexington and Concord, two towns right outside Boston. It is not surprising that the first two battles of the war took place in Massachusetts: In October 1774 General Gage had dismissed the state assembly, and under the leadership of John Hancock, an independent "rebel" government had been established. Meanwhile, minute men (groups of citizens who would be ready to fight at a minute's notice) were organized, and arms were stockpiled at Concord and Lexington. It was these caches of arms that General Gage ordered destroyed in April 1775, but by the time the British arrived at Concord after marching overnight, the minute men had been forewarned of their approach by Paul Revere, who had also ridden through the night. Facing a line of Americans on the Concord village green, the British commander ordered the minute men to drop their weapons, but just then a shot rang out from behind a stone wall and fighting began. This was the gunfire later described as "the shot heard 'round the world," for it set in motion the American Revolution.

The Second Continental Congress

The Second Continental Congress marked, in effect, the meeting of the first national governing body. The delegates created the Continental army headed by the Virginian George Washington, set up councils to negotiate Indian affairs, and sent representatives to Europe. In June 1775 John Dickinson and Thomas Jefferson coauthored the "Declaration on the Causes of Taking Up Arms," in which they insisted that the colonies were not raising armies in order to sever the bond with Britain, nor to be independent, but merely to defend themselves against tyranny. They again pledged their allegiance to King George III while reviling his tyrannical Parliament; however, for the British this division between king and ministry made no sense, for the royal leader and his government were believed to be an indivisible unit. In July 1775 Dickinson authored a final plea for resolution called the "Olive Branch Petition," which reiterated the colonists' desire for peace and reconciliation. But by the time King George received the document, the British had already suffered heavy losses at the Battle of Bunker Hill in June 1775; the King was unwilling to further communicate with the American colonies, whom he considered to be in a state of rebellion.

By the spring of 1776 the British had abandoned Boston to Washington's army, and patriots were making calls for American independence. The most strident of these expressions was articulated by a recent English emigrant, Thomas Paine, who radically challenged the notion that King George was a kindly monarch, denouncing him as the "royal brute" in his pamphlet *Common Sense*. Paine's work, advocating an independent republic run by the people, devoid of king or monarchy, proved to be extremely influential and sold out everywhere in the colonies. By May 1776 the Second Continental Congress had recommended that the states replace their old colonial charters with newly written constitutions, which were eventually to become some of the prototypes for the U.S. Constitution.

The Declaration of Independence

In June 1776 the Second Continental Congress chose five members to draw up the Declaration of Independence from Britain: Thomas Jefferson, Benjamin Franklin, John Adams, Roger Sherman, and Robert Livingston. Jefferson, chosen to author the document, drew from his readings of the Classics and from the works of Enlightenment thinkers such as Jean-Jacques Rousseau and Charles-Louis de Secondat, baron de La Brède et de Montesquieu. But most of all, Jefferson was influenced by the Englishman John Locke's famous *Second Treatise of Government*, which described government as originating in a social compact between a people and their ruler. According to this idea, human beings had certain inalienable, natural rights that the ruler must honor (such as life, liberty, and property). If a king fails to honor these rights, the result is tyranny, and the people should—or even must—sever the compact binding them to their ruler and revolt. Replacing Locke's idea of property with "the pursuit of happiness," the Declaration of Independence begins, "We hold these truths to be self-evident: That all men are created equal; that they are endowed by their Creator with certain unalienable rights; that among these are life, liberty and the pursuit of happiness."

After its adoption on July 4, 1776, the declaration was read from Philadelphia's Independence Hall, and copies were sent to all of the states. Certain issues proved problematic: The paradox of stating that all men were equal while hundreds of thousands of African-Americans were enslaved and deprived of their liberty, did not escape many Northerners. In addition, while declaring that all men were equal, the declaration stated nothing about the rights of women. Nonetheless, despite these glaring contradictions, the declaration was an eloquent and impassioned summary of the greatest political ideals of the Enlightenment.

The Causes of the Revolution: Economic or Ideological?

The Declaration of Independence thus summed up the ideas of liberty that were a fundamental cause of the Revolution. Yet scholars still disagree over how important the ideals of freedom outlined in the declaration were for the average American, as opposed to the issue of excessive taxation. Some scholars argue that the rhetoric of *liberty* and *freedom* was merely a veiled means of arguing for "freedom from taxes." Others suggest that the taxation issue was less significant than fundamental ideological differences with Britain. Additional factors in the desire for independence were Britain's distance from the colonies and the fact that, as time proceeded, the colonists diverged from their British ancestors in speech patterns, cultural mores, and religious practices. In addition, waves of emigrants from Germany, Holland, and Ireland naturally felt no allegiance to Britain whatsoever.

But the ideals of individual liberty and freedom from a tyrannical government were clearly important to many American colonists, even if not for all. By 1775 *liberty* had come to mean not only a general sort of personal freedom but also specifically American liberty from Britain. Throughout the oratory of the American patriots, the term *liberty* invoked notions of self-dependence along with ideas of protest and resistance that vied with the American colonists' shared Protestant ethics. Indeed, one of the reasons why the notion of liberty was so important to the American colonists was that many British politicians thought that the Americans were not entitled to the same liberties that the British were. Although Britain was one of the world's most libertarian states during the eighteenth century, Americans felt that they were not being treated equally, and the American patriots firmly believed that they were entitled to the same liberties as any Englishman.

The Articles of Confederation

The Declaration of Independence, in which the name "the United States of America" was coined for the first time, was followed up by another important document: the Articles of Confederation. The articles were an early constitution, hastily written in the midst of the war (between 1776 and 1777), in which practical matters took precedence over theoretical issues such as sovereignty and states' rights. Primarily, the articles were penned to empower the national body of the newly declared United States to fight a war. John Dickinson wrote much of the early draft, in which Congress had the power to raise taxes via quotas for each state and the western territories were placed under government control. However, Dickinson's initial proposal was opposed by North Carolina's Thomas Burke. Like many Americans, Burke had become innately suspicious of any form of centralized authority. Burke succeeded in introducing a clause preserving state sovereignty and independence, and the resultant document was a weak shadow of Dickinson's early draft. In the final version, Congress was granted control of the armed forces, foreign policy, Indian affairs, coinage, and the postal service, but Congress did not have the power to raise taxes. Although drafted in late 1776 and early 1777, the articles took several years to be ratified by each state, with Maryland holding off until 1781. By this point, it had already become apparent that a stronger national authority was needed to control the country effectively, and there was increasing talk of revising the Articles of Confederation.

Problems with the Articles of Confederation

Some of the strongest arguments for reforming the Articles of Confederation were economic ones. From 1782 on, when peace negotiations with Britain were beginning and through the postwar years, perhaps the two largest problems facing the United States were the large national debt and the continued economic competition posed by British mercantilism. Congress, by the powers delimited in the Articles of Confederation, lacked the power to directly tax citizens and even lacked sufficient funds to pay the interest on the foreign debt. Only by requisitioning taxes from each state could congressional monies be raised. The states generally failed to comply with such requisitions, leaving Congress so bankrupt that the postwar standing army shrank to eighty men. At one point, Congress attempted to raise funds by taxing all foreign imports 5 percent, but on two occasions this measure was blocked by one or another coastal state. Without federal taxing powers, the national debt grew rapidly, endangering the economic stability of the country.

By the end of the American Revolution in 1783, the economy was in dire straits; the war had burdened the nation with local and international debt and left farms and plantations destroyed. The result was a lower agricultural yield that reduced exports and weakened the American economy. Meanwhile, imports rose as Britain dumped her excess manufactures on the American market with offers of easy credit: A trade deficit resulted because what little hard currency was left flowed out of the country for the purchase of imported goods. At the same time, the paper Continental money that had been used to finance the war had devalued so sharply and radically that "it's not worth a Continental" became a common expression.

Under the current Articles of Confederation, a uniform economic foreign policy was difficult to accomplish. The challenge of British trade competition was not being addressed with a coordinated or comprehensive national agenda; rather, each state administration was attempting to cope with the crisis individually and often in different or even conflicting ways. Coastal Rhode Island enacted customs taxes to hinder European imports and encourage local manufacture, but ships merely docked at nearby Connecticut, which lacked excise duties. Thus, the lack of a concerted policy among the states effectively hindered all attempts to stimulate the economy. Instead of working toward a common economic goal, states competed with one another, with the divergent interests of each state occasionally even leading to threats of secession.

The national government was ostensibly placed in charge of interstate disputes, although, in fact, Congress had as little practical control over state disputes as it did over competitive tariffs among the states. Lacking a Supreme Court, Congress had to depend on the state courts to enforce laws because Congress lacked the authority to control disputes between states or to enforce commercial laws.

Shays's Rebellion

The lack of direct legal or taxation powers over individuals led many conservatives to believe that the newly installed populist democracy could be carried too far. These fears were exacerbated by incidents such as the 1786–1787 Shays's Rebellion in which a group of farmers in western Massachusetts armed and organized themselves with the intent of taking over the state government. The farmers were mostly poverty-stricken war veterans who objected to the heavy state taxes that they could not afford to pay. Although a relatively minor incident in terms of actual violence, the rebellion highlighted the need for dramatic economic reform while fanning fears that populist revolts could ensue in the absence of a strong central authority.

In response to class conflicts, state rivalries, and economic issues such as the national debt and the need for central taxation powers, politicians began moving for a radical revision of the flawed Articles of Confederation. Soon after Shays's Rebellion, James Madison proposed a meeting of states to discuss the problems that Virginia was having with Maryland over the navigation of the Potomac River. Although only five states showed up at the Annapolis Convention of 1786, there was enough discussion of amending the Articles of Confederation to enable Alexander Hamilton, the treasury secretary, to call for a meeting the following year to reform them.

The Constitutional Congress

Hamilton thus initiated the seminal Constitutional Congress held in Philadelphia in May 1787, which was attended by fifty-five delegates from every state except Rhode Island. Although the purpose of the congress was ostensibly to revise the existing charter, men such as Hamilton and Madison seemed to have had in mind a total reshaping of the existing power structure in order to create a federal government with strong economic and legislative powers. These men, who came to be known as the Federalists, believed that a powerful federal government would be able to solve the current problems of trade and economics.

In addition to these practical reasons for wishing to strengthen the national government, a strong current of nationalistic feeling was working during the 1780s to counteract state rivalries and class antipathies. Many statesmen, for example, worked to promote nationalism, believing that the best interests of the country lay in its nationhood. Americans came to view their country as young and full of hope and opportunity, in contrast to decaying, corrupt, and aged Europe. While Europe was stagnant, America was changing, and the notion of self-transformation—of the United States as a work in progress—infused American cultural identity. Thus, nationhood became an ideal (if not a reality) to which many aspired, and improved roads, railways, and postal communication brought the distant reaches of the country closer. It was in light of both of these rising cultural forces—nationalism and cogent economic arguments in favor of a strong federal government—that the Constitutional Committee began reinventing the concept of American government.

When the delegates sat down to reframe the Articles of Confederation, they had in mind to enlarge, empower, and ennoble the national government. They wished to create a strong, sovereign power with both local and international clout rather than a collection of states whose divergent interests would constantly compete with another. A republic then, was generally seen as a preferable model to a union, but many thought that the United States was too large an area and too diverse a population for a republican form of government, and clearly a wholly centralized government would be inefficient in so large a country. The challenge was to balance the rights and responsibilities of each state with those of a national body by granting separate powers to each.

Although most of the Atlantic world was monarchical during the eighteenth century, Americans' experiences with Britain had made them wary of royalty, and yet there was also a widespread repulsion to granting unlimited freedom to the people. A strong desire existed to uphold the democratic tradition of the Revolution and to allow the people to rule, but many feared allowing the people unlimited freedoms and wished to devise ways to check the power of the masses. As Hamilton argued, "Give all the power to the many, they will oppress the few. Give all the power to the few, they will oppress the many." The challenge was to grant individuals as much freedom as possible while still checking their ability to gain power or to allow minorities to seize control.

The solution, most delegates agreed, lay in a system of divided government in which the powers of each branch would both check one another and restrain what was seen as the "impulsive" will of the people. Such a system of checks and balances formed by several branches of government had long been advocated by many eighteenth-century thinkers like Locke and Montesquieu and was considered the wisest system of government for the United States.

Writing the Constitution

On the second day of the proceedings, in late May 1787, Edmund Randolph presented the first framework for a constitution to the delegates. Known as the Virginia Resolves and authored primarily by Madison, this plan outlined a national legislature with two arms: one elected by the people and another appointed by the first, along with a strong executive office and a federal judiciary. A couple of weeks later the New Jersey opposition countered by suggesting mere revisions to the existing Articles of Confederation, with its system of equal representation for all states. The congress now had two concrete propositions to compare as well as several state constitutions that served as further models. Thus, although most delegates agreed from the outset on the idea of a tripartite government, their largest concern was balancing the diverse interests of different states. The large states, fearing that they would constantly be vetoed by small states, favored the Virginia Plan's structure of proportional representation, while the smaller states backed the New Jersey Plan, which gave the small states an equal voice.

That summer in Philadelphia it was exceptionally hot, and there were points when consensus seemed an impossible dream. Tempers flared, a few representatives stormed out in anger, and others such as the Virginian Patrick Henry refused to attend at all, claiming that he "smelled a rat." Throughout the entire process, George Washington presided over affairs, and the aging Benjamin Franklin made daily appearances. But then compromises were agreed on. The "three-fifths compromise" was reached: in matters of direct taxes and representation in the House, one slave would be counted as equivalent to three-fifths of one white man. The new Constitution, it was concluded, was to have the power to tax and to regulate commerce, the army, and foreign trade, and states were to retain control of police, schools, local community affairs, and franchise qualifications. A pivotal moment arrived in the compromise over state representation: It was agreed that the legislative branch would consist of a Senate with two senators from each state along with a House of Representatives in which there would be representation proportional to state size.

Creating the executive office proved to be another hurdle because it was difficult for the delegates to conceive of a leader who would not become kinglike in some fashion. To avoid this, there were those who envisioned a three or four man split-presidency, similar to of the Directory established in France after the French Revolution. Some advocated that the president should be elected directly by the people, but aside from Washington, few nationally renowned figures existed. Others wanted the president to be chosen directly by Congress: The objection to this method was that it would leave no division of power between the branches of government. Finally, the rather clumsy solution of the electoral office was agreed on, wherein the people or the state legislature would select electors to represent them in voting for a presidential candidate.

Perhaps one of the most innovative aspects of the Constitution was the power granted to the Supreme Court. The notion of judicial supremacy—that the Supreme Court has the ultimate say in governmental disputes and that its judges are the official interpreters of the Constitution—had little precedent in the contemporary governments of Europe. This notion was to become a central feature of American government.

By the end of July 1787, most of the major aspects of the document had been analyzed, dissected, and finally agreed on. At this point, the proposed Constitution was handed to a committee of James Madison, Alexander Hamilton, William Johnson, Rufus King, and Gouverneur Morris to be written. By early September, the Constitution was completed and signed by almost all of the delegates. Franklin made a speech describing it as a document of compromise, admitting that although it was not perfect, it was "near to perfection." The work of the Constitutional Committee was now over. The next step was to see whether it would be accepted by the people of America—that is, whether the states would ratify it.

The Federalist/Anti-Federalist Debate

In order for the Constitution to go into effect, it needed to be ratified by nine of the thirteen states. Each state was required to have its own special meeting to discuss and vote whether to approve the Constitution. The advocates of the Constitution, who became known as the Federalists, knew that a long, hard struggle was in store for them. The Federalists believed that vast opportunities lay ahead for the United States that demanded the leadership of a strong federal government. However, a large majority of statesmen were still adamantly opposed to strong federal control. Long rhetorical battles proceeded in state legislatures all along the

Atlantic seaboard as the Federalists attempted to win support for the document in which they believed the future of the country rested. It was at this time that Alexander Hamilton, James Madison, and John Jay collaborated on a series of essays, *The Federalist Papers,* which expounded the Federalist cause in an effort to swing public opinion in New York State.

The Federalists, many of whom had been active in framing the Constitution, were a unified group who argued their case cogently and simply. By contrast, the Anti-Federalists were a rather disorganized array of various interest groups who opposed the Constitution for a variety of reasons. Unlike the Federalists, who argued for the Constitution, the Anti-Federalists' objections were necessarily negative; without a viable alternative to present, their battle was a difficult one. The Anti-Federalists included Americans who were opposed to government in general—especially centralized control—and who wished for as little government as possible. Anti-Federalist objections came from many small landowners and rural citizens who saw the Federalists as a wealthy, educated elite attempting to wrest power away from the people. Furthermore, rural people tended to be far more isolated than urban dwellers, so their interests were local; national issues resonated little with them. Although the Anti-Federalists tended to be less educated or wealthy than the Federalists, there was also an Anti-Federalist elite of lawyers and statesmen who objected to the Constitution. Some believed that the United States was too large for a republic. Others thought that a house of representatives comprising a mere fifty-five men was too small to accurately represent the views of such a diverse people. Still others argued that the Constitution would leave the door open for small groups to seize control. A final Anti-Federalist camp comprised those who objected to the document on ethical or ideological grounds. People criticized the Constitution's de facto endorsement of slavery. In addition, many quarters complained that a bill of rights was needed because the Constitution did not adequately protect the rights of the individual. During the ratification debates in New York State, for example, a bill of rights was demanded. Madison's assurances that one would be written as soon as the new government met helped allay fears and ensure ultimate ratification in that state.

The small states of Delaware, Connecticut, and New Jersey ratified quickly, followed by Georgia, which had had a recent Indian uprising that made it eager for national protection. Pennsylvania, New Hampshire, Maryland, and South Carolina had ratified by the spring of 1788, but the long and difficult debates raged in Virginia, New York, and Massachusetts. All three had ratified by 1788; thus, the necessary nine states had been reached, and the Constitution was adopted. George Washington traveled to New York, treated to celebrations on his way, and was sworn in as the first president of the United States. In 1789 North Carolina ratified, followed finally by a reluctant Rhode Island.

One of the most important legacies of the ratification debates was the Anti-Federalists insistence on a bill of rights to safeguard the rights and liberties of the individual; Massachusetts, New York, and New Hampshire had ratified the Constitution only with the stipulation that the Bill of Rights would be added to the document. In 1789 the Bill of Rights was passed as the first ten amendments to the Constitution, specifically articulating the rights of the citizen and limiting the federal government's powers to infringe on individual liberty. One by one, the amendments guarded the individual's right to free speech and assembly, freedom of worship, and freedom from cruel and unusual punishment, unreasonable searches and seizures, and self-incrimination. The Sixth Amendment mandated the right to a public trial, and the Second Amendment guarded the right to bear arms.

Creating Financial Stability in the New Republic

The ten amendments to the Constitution were formally added to the Constitution in 1791, by which time the newly formed government had turned its attention to the economic situation. The nation was still deeply indebted to foreign governments and banks, local banks, state governments, and individuals due to loans procured to finance the War of Independence. The accruing interest on these debts had shortsightedly been met by printing more paper money, which had led to rapid deflation of the currency and of government bonds. In response to this financial crisis, treasury secretary Alexander Hamilton masterminded a series of national economic strategies to recuperate the national debt and still inflation by controlling taxation and customs policies. By the spring of 1790, Hamilton's controversial *Report on Public Credit* had been passed by Congress, and the federal government had assumed responsibility for both federal and state debts accrued over the last decade and a half. Moreover, these debts (state and federal debts to both domestic and international debtors) were to be fully repaid as soon as possible by means of interest-producing government-issued savings bonds. Although many recognized that this repayment was essential for the newly founded nation to develop good credit, it was a time of depression—when most people were bad-mouthing debtors as voracious and greedy and were railing against repayment—and Hamilton's ideas were extremely unpopular. Madison and Jefferson vociferously opposed Hamilton's plan, and the necessary support of the Virginians was gained only through an agreement that the new capital would be moved from Philadelphia to a location on the Potomac on the border between the southern states of Maryland and Virginia—to a city that would later be called Washington, D.C.

Perhaps most central to Hamilton's visionary economic infrastructure was his proposal for a national bank, which met with as much opposition from Madison and Jefferson as his loan repayment scheme had. A state-owned bank supplied by public funds was considered the essential base on which credit, inflation, revenue, and investment would rest. Congress, which recognized that a national bank was the cornerstone of Hamilton's other policies, ultimately passed the bill with Washington's endorsement in late 1790, but not before a bitter fight had ensued between Hamiltonians and the Jefferson/Madison team. A rift developed that was to split Congress into factions of North and South, industry versus agrarianism, and pit the new way against the old.

Jefferson wrote a long opinion for President Washington in which he objected to the conglomeration of power and capital that a national bank would produce and, interpreting the Constitution strictly, concluded that a national bank was unconstitutional. In response, Hamilton argued that a national bank was not only economically beneficial and necessary but was also perfectly justified by the new Constitution. Many of the issues revolving around the creation of a national bank rested on the question of the extent of government power in the public sphere. Jefferson joined Madison in arguing that "to take a single step beyond the boundaries . . . is to take possession of a boundless field of power."

The Emergence of the Two Parties

Ultimately, the National Bank was instituted, with subscription to its stocks beginning in August 1791. It succeeded in allowing for the full repayment of the national debt and in establishing excellent credit for the United States. However, the congressional debates over the National Bank are seen by historians as the origin for the split that led to the development of the two major parties in the United States. Hamilton and his Federalist allies, who primarily represented the interests of the commercial, industrial North, are considered the predecessors of the current Republican Party. Hamilton's opponents, Madison and Jefferson, who represented the interests of the agrarian South, were called the Anti-Federalists (later known as the Democrat-Republicans), and they developed into the current Democratic Party.

The years of Washington's presidency were characterized by the rift that emerged between the Hamiltonian Federalists and their opponents, the Democrat-Republicans. The French Revolution of 1789 particularly served to entrench these differences. The United States avoided becoming entangled in the European war of 1793, but internal politics suffered as Americans were starkly divided on the issue of the French Revolution. After having supported the Americans during their revolution with troops and funds, the French expected reciprocal assistance, but Washington feared that America was too young a country to bear the strain of war and declared neutrality. Although Hamilton and the Federalists had advised a neutral course, the Anti-Federalists felt that the United States should support France. Democrat-Republican societies, whose members perceived themselves to be the descendants of the Revolutionary-era Sons of Liberty in upholding the ideals of populist democracy, were formed in opposition to the Washington administration.

Party conflict intensified during the presidency of John Adams, who replaced Washington in 1796. Although today one assumes the existence, even the necessity, of a strong opposition party to be requisite in a democracy, during the eighteenth century people believed that in a government of the people, the existence of an opposition party signaled the presence of large malcontent elements of the population. In 1798, the Adams administration thus passed the Alien and Sedition Acts, which lengthened the residency time required for naturalization of immigrants from five to fourteen years and restricted free speech and writing by making public criticism of the government illegal. These acts were largely an attempt to silence Democrat-Republican newspaper editors, many of whom were foreign born. However, the sedition acts were hugely unpopular and were quickly attacked as an unconstitutional violation of the right to free speech.

In 1801, when Jefferson succeeded Adams as the nation's third president, the country was still racked by factionalism, and many feared that his sympathies with the French Jacobins would lead him to institute a form of radical democracy. These fears proved unfounded; Jefferson took a path of moderation, attempting to unite both Federalist and Anti-Federalist factions.

Native American Histories: Seventeenth-Century Hostilities

The history of the founding of America involved not only war with Britain and the formation of political and economic institutions; it also involved violent conflict with the original inhabitants of North America. The Indians initially enjoyed excellent relations with the earliest white settlers during the seventeenth century. Early reports indicate that the Native Americans first encountered along the Atlantic seaboard taught the settlers how to grow squash, corn, and tobacco, and soon a profitable fur trade was established. However, this genial period soon gave way to mutual distrust and suspicion that erupted in outbreaks of violence as early as the 1630s. The Pequot War, for example, grew out of a couple of Pequot attacks on white traders in 1635 and 1637, which incited the Massachusetts governor, John Endecott, to destroy two entire Pequot villages. In turn, the Pequot attacked Wethersfield, Connecticut, killing nine people. In a cycle of escalating violence, the whites responded by recruiting Niantic and Narragansett Indians to add to a large New England militia force that attacked the Pequot stronghold, killing over five hundred Pequot men, women, and children.

Other attacks and counterattacks between white settlers and the Algonquian occurred throughout the 1640s near the Dutch territory of New Amsterdam (New York), and Virginia was the site of continuous violence throughout the second half of the seventeenth century. King Philip's War, which raged around Boston in 1676, arose out of conflicts between Algonquian converted to Christianity and traditional Algonquian. Whites had murdered Algonquian thought to have killed an Algonquian convert, and bloody battles between the Massachusetts militia and bands of Algonquian lasted for over a year. This war strongly affected the small population of New Englanders, who lost nearly 20 percent of their males in the fighting, and entrenched the increasing hatred between Native Americans and New Englanders.

Eighteenth-Century Conflicts

By the first half of the eighteenth century, several tribes (the Iroquois, Creek, and Cherokee) had allied themselves with Britain, hoping that the British would protect them from the invasive American colonists who were constantly pushing westward onto Indian lands. Their hopes were somewhat justified because the British did make efforts to stay westward expansion. In October 1763, after the British won the Seven Years' War and expelled the French, Britain proclaimed that all the land west of the Allegheny Mountains was Native American and off limits to white expansion. However, British efforts proved to be little more than a temporary measure, for the "Great Proclamation" ignored the reality of Native Americans living to the east of this border as well as the many white Americans who were settled to the west of this line. Predictably, in less than a decade the proclamation was adjusted to allow for white settlement in western Pennsylvania and other areas.

Other tribes, such as the Ottawa, had no desire for paternalistic British protection and challenged these British territorial claims. In 1760 the Ottawa chief Pontiac (a former French ally) gathered a large force of various tribes and attacked forts all along the western frontier. He captured several forts and killed about 200 people but was unable to breach the defences of Fort Duquesne. After three years of conflict with British troops, he agreed to a peace treaty in 1763. Meanwhile, also in 1763, an immigrant gang of Scotch and Irish men called the Paxton Boys went on a rampage against the Indians, massacring 140 Native American converts in one attack alone. Threatening to storm Philadelphia and kill the Quakers, whom they viewed as "Indian-lovers," they were finally dispersed at gunpoint by the Pennsylvania militia.

After unsuccessful attempts by various Native American tribes to repel the British, the Algonquian ceded a large area of land west of the proclamation line to the British in 1768 in the Treaty of Fort Stanwix, which was negotiated by William Johnson, the British commissioner of Indian Affairs for the northern region. In 1769 and 1770 the British commissioner for the southern district, John Stuart, negotiated two similar treaties that similarly carved up the land south of the Ohio River, ceding large tracts to the British and smaller tracts to various indigenous Native American tribes.

The Native Americans and the American Revolution

Most of the Native American tribes had remained neutral during the Revolution, but those who did ally themselves with the British were generally not engaged militarily, as Native American war tactics were largely incompatible with those of the British. Although some tribes, such as the Cherokee in the south, capitalized on the war to attack border settlements, the general lack of unity among the diverse tribes prevented the Native Americans from posing a serious challenge to the Americans during their fight for independence.

The Post-Revolutionary Settlement of the West

Soon after the Treaty of Paris officially cemented the American victory and granted sovereignty to the former colonists, the U.S. government looked to the issue of western expansion. In 1784 Congress began a series of talks and negotiations with various Native American leaders in an effort to secure more lands for white settlers by pushing the Indians out of their ancestral lands and relocating them farther west. The United States signed a treaty at Fort Stanwix with the Iroquois in 1784 and one with the Cherokee and Creek in South Carolina in 1785. In both of these treaties, Native American chiefs signed over vast portions of land. Nonetheless, despite these concessions, the subsequent years saw continued and frequent skirmishes between settlers and other tribes, such as the Shawnee, Delaware, and Miami, who refused to allow the whites to invade their land and intermittently attacked settlers.

By the late 1780s the western tribes, who had previously been led by the powerful Iroquois Confederacy, organized themselves into a western confederacy of tribes led by the Miami. In October 1790 and again in 1791 at Fort Wayne, U.S. forces suffered defeats at the hands of the Western Confederacy, which included the five-thousand-strong Creek army. The Western Confederacy's term for peace was the halting of white expansion at the Ohio River. Refusing to accept this boundary, the United States retaliated by sending a large force to crush the tribes in August 1794 at the Battle of Fallen Timbers in Ohio. The following year, 1795, the United States signed a treaty with the defeated Western Confederacy in which it staked its claim to most of present-day Ohio but acknowledged the Native Americans' claims to sovereignty by right of occupation to all of the land not yet ceded. In fact, however, claims to Indian land continued throughout the subsequent years since most whites felt that the Native Americans must either assimilate or move west. As conflict with the whites increased and game decreased, many nomadic Indian tribes were indeed forced to follow the diminishing herds out west, and others tried to survive by settling down and adopting white culture and religion.

After the wars of the 1790s, a period of relative calm existed before the next major conflicts surfaced in 1811, when the Shawnee chief Tecumseh and his orator brother, the Prophet, aligned themselves with the British in an effort to challenge American power along the western frontier. Tecumseh and the Prophet worked tirelessly to unite the western tribes and conglomerate their defenses in order to create a vertical strip that would run from Canada to the American South. They succeeded in forging a Creek-Shawnee alliance that attacked groups of western settlers in 1811 and 1812, wreaking such havoc that Major General Andrew Jackson was called in to quell the violence.

Jackson, a ruthless enemy of the Native Americans, fought a vicious war with the Creek tribe, shooting whole villages of hundreds of civilians. After several months he succeeded in breaching the formidable Creek fortress at Horseshoe Bend and killing nearly all of the one thousand inhabitants. Crushed, the remaining Creek were forced to surrender half their lands, comprising more than half of Alabama and part of Georgia. Wars such as this made it clear that the western settlers were not moving into unoccupied lands but were actively colonizing the North American continent.

The Nineteenth Century: A Tragic Conclusion

By the first decade of the nineteenth century the numbers of Native Americans had been dramatically decreased through starvation, disease, and forced removal. After 1814 Native Americans lacked their British allies due to an Anglo-American peace agreement that had been reached at the conclusion of the 1812 war with Britain. Without their British protection, the tribes progressively lost more and more lands. In 1819, for example, 6 million acres in current-day Michigan were signed away under the Treaty of Saginaw. A few years later, in 1826, Michigan's Governor General Lewis Cass procured more lands at a conference at Prairie du Chien by forcing dozens of tribes to make independent deals with him. The once-powerful Miami sold their Indiana territories for fifty-five thousand dollars and an annuity of twenty-five thousand dollars, and the Potawatomi, too, relinquished their chunk of Indiana. In the following years, more and more Indian lands were sold, ceded, or claimed as American territory after victorious battles; by 1830 almost all of the remaining tribes had been forced west of the Mississippi. In 1832 the Sauk chief Black Hawk tried to rally tribes to unite against the Americans, but he failed and the result was merely that more land in Illinois was signed away for white settlement.

Even the Cherokee, who had settled in Georgia in 1826, built towns; held elections; established a supreme court, schools, and industry; and had drawn up a constitution based on the American model, were all forcibly removed and were relocated by 1835. Their independent nation, it was argued, violated the U.S. Constitution's sovereignty, but it was no doubt also the discovery of gold on Cherokee lands that portended their demise. A rush of prospectors lobbied for the removal of the Cherokee, and in the landmark 1830 *Cherokee Nation v. Georgia,* the Cherokee fought for their freedom by arguing for their status as a separate nation, only to have their claims formally dismissed. Other members of the so-called Five Civilized Peoples (Choctaw, Cherokee, Chickasaw, Creek, and Seminole tribes), who had a long history of village life, also attempted to survive by adapting to European norms and founding towns. But pressure for their removal increased, and after Jackson became president in 1829, their downfall was similarly imminent.

Throughout the 1830s, under President Jackson's Indian Removal Act, tens of thousands of Native Americans were uprooted and marched west, with thousands dying from hardships and hunger on the long journeys. In Florida, the Seminole Indians refused to leave and were killed in large numbers. The Cherokee spoke of their relocation as "the Trail of Tears." By the mid–nineteenth century, Native Americans, their numbers decimated by European diseases, alcohol, war, and starvation, had been mostly confined to reservations in western and southwestern portions of the country.

The treatment of the Native Americans raises problematic

questions regarding the ideas of liberty that were central to the founding of America. Indeed, the ideals so eloquently articulated in the Constitution and the Bill of Rights—ideals of personal liberty and justice, and of freedom of speech and religion—were generally not extended to Native Americans, African Americans, and often not even to white women. And yet the Constitution, despite its contradictions, contained a blueprint for one of the most free and just societies in the world. Over the course of two hundred years, Americans would fight to extend the rights and freedoms outlined by the founding fathers to all Americans, often fighting bloody wars to do so. And despite its imperfections, the American ideals of democracy would prove to be an enduring legacy that has not only survived for more than two centuries but has also been a major influence on political systems throughout the world.

GREAT
SPEECHES
IN
HISTORY

The
Colonists
Resist
British Rule

General Search Warrants Are Illegal and Unjust

James Otis Jr.

Since the seventeenth century, Britain had imposed certain trade restrictions on the American colonies in order to ensure that British industry flourished. These laws, which comprised the Navigation Act of 1651 and the Enumerated Commodities Act of 1660, have been a point of great contention among historians: Some historians argue that British control of trade and shipping was the primary cause of the American desire for independence, while others argue that independence was unavoidable and that mercantile concerns were merely one of various factors that compelled the colonists down the path toward inevitable independence. In general, though, most historians agree that prior to the 1760s, these navigation laws were not an important issue—largely because most of the colonists completely ignored them and smuggled, pirated, and traded illegally with the peoples of the Caribbean and other regions. In colonial America, smuggling was considered a necessary, and even respectable, profession.

Throughout the late 1750s, while Britain was at war with France in North America, the American colonists supplied the French with supplies. These blatant offenses incited the British authorities to rigorously enforce their trade laws. Following a precedent in British law, they stepped up their customs controls, granting customs officials the right to search for smuggled goods anywhere and anytime they wanted. These

From James Otis Jr., "On the Writs of Assistance," address to the Superior Court of Boston, Massachusetts, February 1761, as reprinted in *Orations of American Orators*, rev. ed., vol. 1 (New York: Cooperative Publication Society, 1900).

warrants to search any ship and any home for illegal goods were called "Writs of Assistance."

The writs were granted for the lifetime of the king, so when King George died in 1760, the British customs officials had to reapply for them. At this time, the advocate general of Massachusetts (representing the British Crown) was James Otis Jr., whose job it would have been to legally uphold the writs. However, Otis considered the writs to be a flagrant violation of personal liberty, arguing that "a man's house is his castle." Otis resigned his post and delivered the following speech in the Massachusetts Superior Court. Otis contends that "special" writs, which allow searches of suspects' homes, are legal. The Writs of Assistance, however, are "general," allowing unlimited searches, and are therefore illegal. Originally, this was a five-hour speech, but all that remains is this section, which was transcribed several years later.

In fact, the writs were technically legal because the British Crown had supreme control over the colonies. However, according to John Quincy Adams, who would later become the president of the United States, this speech was important because it marked the beginning of the founding of America. Adams was among the people listening to Otis that February day, and years later, looking back on the event, he described Otis's speech as "the first scene of the first act of opposition to the arbitrary claims of Great Britain. . . . American independence was then and there born."

May it Please Your Honors: I was desired by one of the court to look into the books, and consider the question now before them concerning writs of assistance. I have accordingly considered it, and now appear not only in obedience to your order, but likewise in behalf of the inhabitants of this town, who have presented another petition, and out of regard to the liberties of the subject. And I take this opportunity to declare, that whether under a fee or not (for in such a cause as this I despise a fee), I will to my dying day oppose with all the powers and faculties God has given me, all such instruments of slavery on the one hand, and villany on the other, as this writ of assistance is.

Writs Are a Form of Tyranny

It appears to me the worst instrument of arbitrary power, the most destructive of English liberty and the fundamental principles of law, that ever was found in an English law-book. I must therefore beg your honors' patience and attention to the whole range of an argument, that may perhaps appear uncommon in many things, as well as to points of learning that are more remote and unusual; that the whole tendency of my design may the more easily be perceived, the conclusions better descend, and the force of them be better felt. I shall not think much of my pains in this cause, as I engaged in it from principle. I was solicited to argue this cause as advocate-general; and because I would not, I have been charged with desertion from my office. To this charge I can give a very sufficient answer. I renounced that office, and I argue this cause from the same principle; and I argue it with the greater pleasure, as it is in favor of British liberty, at a time when we hear the greatest monarch upon earth declaring from his throne that he glories in the name of Briton, and that the privileges of his people are dearer to him than the most valuable prerogatives of his crown; and as it is in opposition to a kind of power, the exercise of which in former periods of history cost one king of England his head, and another his throne. I have taken more pains in this cause than I ever will take again, although my engaging in this and another popular cause has raised much resentment. But I think I can sincerely declare, that I cheerfully submit myself to every odious name for conscience' sake; and from my soul I despise all those whose guilt, malice, or folly has made them my foes. Let the consequences be what they will, I am determined to proceed. The only principles of public conduct, that are worthy of a gentleman or a man, are to sacrifice estate, ease, health, and applause, and even life, to the sacred calls of his country.

These manly sentiments, in private life, make the good

citizens; in public life, the patriot and the hero. I do not say that, when brought to the test, I shall be invincible. I pray God I may never be brought to the melancholy trial, but if ever I should, it will be then known how far I can reduce to practice principles which I know to be founded in truth. In the mean time I will proceed to the subject of this writ.

These Writs Are Illegal

Your honors will find in the old books concerning the office of a justice of the peace, precedents of general warrants to search suspected houses. But in more modern books, you will find only special warrants to search such and such houses, specially named, in which the complainant has before sworn that he suspects his goods are concealed; and will find it adjudged, that special warrants only are legal. In the same manner I rely on it, that the writ prayed for in this petition, being general, is illegal. It is a power that places the liberty of every man in the hands of every petty officer. I say I admit that special writs of assistance, to search special places, may be granted to certain persons on oath; but I deny that the writ now prayed for can be granted, for I beg leave to make some observations on the writ itself, before I proceed to other acts of Parliament. In the first place, the writ is universal, being directed "to all and singular justices, sheriffs, constables, and all other officers and subjects"; so that, in short, it is directed to every subject in the King's dominions. Everyone with this writ may be a tyrant; if this commission be legal, a tyrant in a legal manner, also, may control, imprison, or murder anyone within the realm. In the next place, it is perpetual, there is no return. A man is accountable to no person for his doings. Every man may reign secure in his petty tyranny, and spread terror and desolation around him, until the trump of the archangel shall excite different emotions in his soul. In the third place, a person with his writ, in the daytime, may enter all houses, shops, etc., at will, and command all to assist him. Fourthly, by this writ, not only deputies, etc., but even their menial servants, are allowed to lord it over us. What is this but to have the curse of Canaan with a witness on us; to be the servant of servants, the most despicable of God's creation? Now one of the most essential branches of English liberty is the freedom of one's house. A man's house is his castle; and whilst he is quiet, he is as well guarded as a prince in his castle. This writ, if it should be declared legal, would totally annihilate this privilege. Custom-house officers may enter our houses when they please; we are commanded to permit their entry. Their menial servants may enter, may break locks, bars, and everything in their way; and whether they break through malice or revenge, no man, no court can inquire. Bare suspicion without oath is sufficient. This wanton exercise of this power is not a chimerical suggestion of a heated brain. I will mention some facts. Mr. Pew [customs officer] had one of these writs, and when Mr. Ware [customs officer] succeeded him, he endorsed this writ over to Mr. Ware; so that these writs are negotiable from one officer to another; and so your honors have no opportunity of judging the persons to whom this vast power is delegated. Another instance is this: Mr. Justice Walley had called this same Mr. Ware before him, by a constable, to answer for a breach of the Sabbath-day acts, or that of profane swearing. As soon as he had finished, Mr. Ware asked him if he had done. He replied, "Yes." "Well then," said Mr. Ware, "I will show you a little of my power. I command you to permit me to search your house for uncustomed goods"; and went on to search the house from the garret to the cellar; and then served the constable in the same manner! But to show another absurdity in this writ: if it should be established, I insist upon it every person, by the 14th Charles II, has this power as well as the custom-house officers. The words are: "It shall be lawful for any person or persons authorized," etc. What a scene does this open! Every man prompted by revenge, ill-humor, or wantonness to inspect the inside of his neighbor's house, may get a writ of assistance. Others will ask it from self-defence; one arbitrary exertion will provoke another, until society be involved in tumult and in blood.

British Policies Are Arbitrary and Unconstitutional

Joseph Warren

During the infamous Boston massacre of March 1770, five rioting Bostonians were shot and killed by British soldiers. In March 1772, when a young doctor named Joseph Warren gave the following commemorative speech, the massacre was still fresh in the memory of the people, and Boston had become the center of anti-British sentiment. In this politically charged atmosphere, public orations were a popular means of debating the increasingly problematic relationship with Britain and of addressing the series of unpopular laws and taxes that were seen to impinge on colonial liberties. Without American representation in the British Parliament, there seemed to be no way to check Britain's power: Taxes could be raised repeatedly, and various restrictive laws could be passed. In this atmosphere, the question of how to secure freedom and prevent tyranny loomed large.

This oration is essentially a legal argument, wherein Warren enumerates the ways in which Britain has acted unconstitutionally; namely, by placing internal taxes on the Americans and by bringing a standing army into Boston during peacetime. Warren argues that the deaths of the five Bostonians resulted because the British had resorted to force to deal with a civil conflict. He contends that a standing army contradicts the very notion of civilized institutions of debate and negotiation, and he appeals to the British tradition of liberty and love of reason as the

From Joseph Warren, "Constitutional Liberty and Arbitrary Power," address delivered to the public in Boston, Massachusetts, March 5, 1772, as reprinted in *Early American Orations, 1760–1824*, edited by Louie R. Heller (New York: Macmillan, 1902).

proper means with which to deal with the current conflict.

In his final lines, Warren argues that it was the love of liberty that persuaded the first settlers to journey to America, and he expresses this hope: "May our land be a land of liberty, the seat of virtue, the asylum of the oppressed." In this way, Warren berates Britain while also challenging the American colonists to create a place where violations of liberty are not tolerated and where problems are dealt with through discussion and reason, not gunfire.

I n young and new-formed communities the grand design of [civil government] is most generally understood and the most strictly guarded; the motives which urged to the social compact cannot be at once forgotten, and that equality which is remembered to have subsisted so lately among them prevents those who are clothed with authority from attempting to invade the freedom of their brethren; or, if such an attempt be made, it prevents the community from suffering the offender to go unpunished; every member feels it to be his interest, and knows it to be his duty to preserve inviolate the constitution on which the public safety depends, and he is equally ready to assist the magistrate in the execution of the laws and the subject in defense of his right, and so long as this noble attachment to a constitution, founded on free and benevolent principles, exists in full vigor, in any state, that state must be flourishing and happy. . . .

The Importance of a Constitution

It was this attachment to a Constitution, founded on free and benevolent principles, which inspired the first settlers of this country,—they saw with grief the daring outrages committed on the free Constitution of their native land,—they knew nothing but a civil war could, at any time, restore its pristine purity. So hard was it to resolve to imbrue their hands in the blood of their brethren, that they chose rather to quit their fair possessions and seek another habitation in a distant clime. When they came to this new world, which they fairly purchased of the Indian natives, the only rightful proprietors, they cultivated the then barren soil by their incessant labor, and defended their clear-bought possession with the fortitude of the Christian and the bravery of the hero.

After various struggles, which, during the tyrannic reigns of the house of Stuart [English monarchs], were constantly kept up between right and wrong, between liberty and slavery, the connection between Great Britain and this colony was settled in the reign of King William and Queen Mary by a compact, the conditions of which were expressed in a charter, by which all the liberties and immunities of British subjects were confided to this province, as fully and as absolutely as they possibly could be by any human instrument which can be devised. And it is undeniably true that the greatest and most important right of a British subject is that he shall be governed by no laws but those to which he, either in person or by his representatives, hath given his consent; and this, I will venture to assert, is the great basis of British freedom; it is interwoven with the Constitution, and whenever this is lost, the Constitution must be destroyed.

The British Constitution, of which ours is a copy, is a happy compound of the three forms, under some of which all governments may be ranged; namely, monarchy, aristocracy, and democracy; of these three the British legislature is composed, and without the consent of each branch, nothing can carry with it the force of a law; but when a law is to be passed for raising a tax, that law can originate only in the democratic branch, which is the House of Commons in Britain and the House of Representatives here. The reason is obvious: they and their constituents are to pay much the largest part of it; but as the aristocratic branch, which in Britain is the House of Lords and in this province the Council, are also to pay some part, their consent is necessary; and as the monarchic branch which in Britain is the King, and with us either the King in person or the Governor whom he shall be pleased to appoint in his stead, is supposed to have a just sense of his own interest, which is that of all the subjects in general, his consent is also necessary, and when the consent of these three branches is obtained, the taxation is most certainly legal.

Let us now allow ourselves a few moments to examine the late acts of the British Parliament for taxing America. Let us with candor judge whether they are constitutionally binding upon us; if they are, in the name of justice let us submit to them, without one murmuring word.

First, I would ask whether the members of the British House of Commons are the democracy of this province? if they are, they are either the people of this province or are elected by the people of this province to represent them, and have, therefore, a constitutional right to originate a bill for taxing them; it is most certain they are neither, and therefore nothing done by them can be said to be done by the democratic branch of our Constitution. I would next ask whether the lords who compose the aristocratic branch of the Legislature are *peers of America*. I never heard it was (even in these extraordinary times) so much as pretended; and if they are not, certainly no act of theirs can be said to be an act of the aristocratic branch of our Constitution. The power of the monarchic branch we, with pleasure, acknowledge resides in the King, who may act either in person or by his representative; and I freely confess that I can see no reason why a proclamation for raising revenues in America, issued by the King's sole authority, would not be equally consistent with our own Constitution, and therefore equally binding upon us with the late acts of the British Parliament for taxing us; for it is plain that if there is any validity in those acts, it must arise altogether from the monarchical branch of the Legislature; and I further think that it would be, at least, as equitable; for I do not conceive it to be of the least importance to us by whom our property is taken away, so long as it is taken without our consent; and I am very much at a loss to know by what figure of rhetoric the inhabitants of this province can be called free subjects, when they are obliged to obey implicitly such laws as are made for them by men three thousand miles off, whom they know not, and whom they never empowered to act for them, or how they can be said to have property, when a body of men over whom they have not the least control, and who are not in any way accountable to them, shall oblige them to deliver up part, or the whole of their substance, without even asking their consent; and yet, whoever pretends that the late acts of the British Parliament for taxing America ought to be deemed binding upon us, must admit at once that we are absolute slaves, and have no property of our own; or else that we may be freemen, and at the same time under the necessity of obeying the arbitrary command of those over whom we have no control or influence, and that we may have property of our own, which is entirely at the disposal of another. Such gross absurdities, I believe, will not be relished in this enlightened age, and it can be no matter of wonder that the people quickly perceived and seriously complained of the inroads which these acts must unavoidably make upon their liberty, and of the hazard to which their whole property is, by them, exposed; for if they may be taxed without their consent, even in the smallest trifle, they may also, without their consent, be deprived of everything they possess, although never so valuable, never so dear. Certainly it never entered the hearts of our ancestors that after so many dangers in this then desolate wilderness, their hard-earned property should be at the disposal of the British Parliament; and as it was soon found that this taxation could not be supported by reason and argument, it seemed necessary that one act of oppression should be enforced by another, and therefore contrary to our just rights as possessing, or at least having a just title to possess, all the liberties and immunities of British subjects, a standing army was established among us in time of peace; and evidently for the purpose of effecting that, which it was one principal design of the founders of the Constitution to prevent when they declared a standing army in a time of peace to be against law; namely, for the enforcement of obedience to acts which, upon fair examination, appeared to be unjust and unconstitutional.

The ruinous consequences of standing armies may be seen in the histories of Syracuse, Rome, and many other once flourishing states, some of which have now scarce a name! Their baneful influence is most suddenly felt, when they are placed in populous cities; for, by a corruption of morals, the public happiness is immediately affected; and that this is one of the effects of quartering troops in a populous city is a truth to which many a mourning parent, many a lost, despairing child in this metropolis, must bear a very melancholy testimony. Soldiers are also taught to consider arms as the only arbiters by which every dispute is to be decided between contending states; they are instructed implicitly to obey their commanders, without inquiring into the justice of the cause they are engaged to support; hence it is, that they are ever to be dreaded as the ready engines of tyranny and oppression. And it is too observable that they are prone to introduce the same mode of decision in the disputes of individuals, from thence have often arisen great animosities between them and the inhabitants, who, whilst in a naked, defenseless state, are frequently insulted and abused by an armed soldiery. And this will be more especially the case when the troops are informed that the intention of their being stationed in any city is to overawe the inhabitants. That this was the avowed design of stationing an armed force in this town is sufficiently known; and we, my fellow-citizens, have seen, we have felt the tragical effects. The fatal fifth of March, 1770, can never be forgotten. The horrors of that dreadful night are but too deeply impressed on our hearts. Language is too feeble to paint the emotions of our souls, when our streets were stained with the blood of our brethren, when our ears were wounded by the groans of the dying, and our eyes were tormented with the sight of the mangled bodies of the dead. When our alarmed imagination presented to our view our houses wrapt in flames, our children subjected to the barbarous caprice of a raging soldiery, our beauteous virgins exposed to all the insolence of unbridled passion, our virtuous wives, endeared to us by every tender tie, falling a sacrifice to worse than brutal violence, and perhaps like the famed Lucretia, distracted with anguish and despair, ending their wretched lives by their own fair hands. When we beheld the authors of our distress parading in our streets, or drawn up in a regular *battalia*, as though in a hostile city, our hearts beat to arms; we snatched our weapons, almost resolved by one decisive stroke to avenge the death of our slaughtered brethren, and to secure from future danger all that we held most dear; but propitious heaven forbade the bloody carnage and saved the threatened victims of our too keen resentment, not by their discipline, not by their regular array,—no, it was royal George's livery that proved their shield,—it was that which turned the pointed engines of destruction from their breasts. The thoughts of vengeance were soon buried in our inbred affection to Great Britain, and calm reason dictated a method of removing the troops, more mild than an immediate resource to the sword. With united efforts you urged the immediate departure of the troops from the town; you urged it with a resolution which insured success; you obtained your wishes, and the removal of the troops was effected without one drop of their blood being shed by the inhabitants.

The immediate actors in the tragedy of that night were surrendered to justice. It is not mine to say how far they were guilty. They have been tried by the country, and acquitted of murder. And they are not to be again arraigned at an earthly bar; but surely the men who have promiscuously scattered death amidst the innocent inhabitants of a populous city ought to see well to it that they are prepared to stand at the bar of an Omniscient Judge! And all who contrived or encouraged the stationing of troops in this place, have reasons of eternal importance to reflect with deep contrition on their base designs, and humbly to repent of their base machinations.

The infatuation which hath seemed, for a number of years, to prevail in the British councils, with regard to us, is truly astonishing! What can be proposed by the repeated attacks made upon our freedom, I really cannot surmise, even leaving justice and humanity out of the question. I do not know one single advantage which can arise to the British nation from our being enslaved:—I know not of any gains which can be wrung from us by oppression, which they may not obtain from us by our own consent, in the smooth channel of commerce; we wish the wealth and prosperity of Britain; we contribute largely to both. Doth what we contribute lose all its value, because it is done voluntarily? The amazing increase of riches to Britain, the great rise of the value of her lands, the flourishing state of her navy, are striking proofs of the advantages derived to her from her commerce with the Colonies; and it is our earnest desire that she may still continue to enjoy the same emoluments, until her streets are paved with American gold; only let us have the pleasure of calling it our own, while it is in our hands; but this, it seems, is too great a favor—we are to be governed by the absolute command of others; our property is to be taken away without our consent; if we complain, our complaints are treated with contempt; if we assert our rights, that assertion is deemed insolence; if we humbly offer to submit the matter to the impartial decision of reason, the sword is judged the most proper argument to silence our murmurs! But this cannot long be the case—surely the British nation will not suffer the reputation of their justice and their honor to be thus sported away by a capricious ministry; no, they will in a short time open their eyes to their true interest; they nourish in their breasts a noble love of liberty; they hold her dear, and they know that all who have once possessed her charms had rather die than suffer her to be torn from their embraces; they are also sensible that Britain is so deeply interested in the prosperity of the Colonies that she must eventually feel every wound given to their freedom; they cannot be ignorant that more dependence may be placed on the affections of a brother than on the forced service of a slave; they must approve your efforts for the preservation of your rights; from a sympathy of soul they must pray for your success; and I doubt not but they will ere long exert themselves effectually to redress your grievances. Even the dissolute reign of Charles II, when the House of Commons impeached the Earl of Clarendon of high treason, the first article on which they founded their accusation was that "he had designed a standing army to be raised, and to govern the kingdom thereby." And the eighth article was that "he had introduced an arbitrary government into his Majesty's plantation"—a terrifying example to those who are now forging chains for this country!

You have, my friends and countrymen, frustrated the designs of your enemies by your unanimity and fortitude; it was your union and determined spirit which expelled those troops who polluted your streets with innocent blood. You have appointed this anniversary as a standard memorial of the bloody consequences of placing an armed force in a populous force, and of your deliverance from the dangers which then seemed to hang over your heads; I am confident that you never will betray the least want of spirit when called upon to guard your freedom. None but they who set a just value upon the blessings of liberty are worthy to enjoy her— your illustrious fathers were her zealous votaries—when the blasting frowns of tyranny drove her from public view, they clasped her in their arms, they cherished her in their generous bosoms, they brought her safe over the rough ocean, and fixed her seat in this then dreary wilderness; they nursed her infant age with the most tender care; for her sake they patiently bore the severest hardships; for her support they underwent the most rugged toils; in her defence they boldly encountered the most alarming dangers; neither the ravenous beast that ranged the woods for prey, nor the more furious savages of the wilderness, could damp their ardor. Whilst with one hand they broke the stubborn glebe, with the other they grasped their weapons, ever ready to protect her from danger. No sacrifice, not even their own blood, was esteemed too rich a libation for her altar! God prospered their valor; they preserved her brilliancy unsullied; they enjoyed her whilst they lived; and, dying, bequeathed the dear inheritance to your care. And as they left you this glorious legacy, they have undoubtedly transmitted to you some portion of their noble spirit, to inspire you with virtue to merit her and courage to preserve her; you surely cannot, with such examples before your eyes, as every page of the history of this country affords, suffer your liberties to be ravished from you by lawless force, or cajoled away by flattery and fraud.

The voice of your fathers' blood cries to you from the ground, My sons, scorn to be slaves! In vain we met the frowns of tyrants—in vain we crossed the boisterous ocean, found a new world, and prepared it for the happy residence of liberty—in vain we toiled—in vain we fought—we bled in vain, if you, our offspring, want valor to repel the assaults of her invaders! Stain not the glory of your worthy ancestors, but like them resolve never to part with your birthright; be wise in your deliberations, and determined in your exertions for the preservation of your liberties. Follow not the dictates of passion, but enlist yourselves under the sacred banner of reason; use every method in your power to secure your rights; at least prevent the curses of posterity from being heaped upon your memories.

If you, with united zeal and fortitude, oppose the torrent of oppression; if you feel the true fire of patriotism burning in your breasts; if you, from your souls, despise the most gaudy dress that slavery can wear; if you really prefer the lonely cottage (whilst blest with liberty) to gilded palaces, surrounded with the ensigns of slavery, you may have the fullest assurance that tyranny, with her whole accursed train, will hide their hideous heads in confusion, shame, and despair; if you perform your part, you must have the strongest confidence that the same Almighty Being who protected your pious and venerable forefathers, who enabled them to turn a barren wilderness into a fruitful field, who so often made bare his arm for their salvation, will still be mindful of you, their offspring.

May this Almighty Being graciously preside in all our councils! May He direct us to such measures as He himself shall approve and be pleased to bless! May we ever be a people favored of God! May our land be a land of liberty, the seat of virtue, the asylum of the oppressed, a name and a praise in the whole earth, until the last shock of time shall bury the empires of the world in one common undistinguished ruin!

Americans Should Oppose British Tyranny

John Hancock

In March 1774, John Hancock, one of the wealthiest merchants in Boston and a longtime opponent of British policies, was chosen to give the commemorative speech at the fourth anniversary of the Boston massacre, speaking exactly two years after Joseph Warren delivered an impassioned speech. The differences between Warren's and Hancock's tone and approach reveal the escalating tensions of the intervening two years. While Warren presented legal and constitutional arguments in favor of the American colonists, Hancock openly denounces the British, arguing that they not only are transgressing legal codes, but are also acting in an outrightly tyrannical fashion.

When Hancock delivered the following speech, it had been a mere three months since tensions had reached the crisis point of the Boston Tea Party. This infamous event was the colonists' reaction to King George's insistent taxing of imported tea. After Britain imposed a new set of duties on British tea in mid-1773, the Americans renewed their smuggling of cheaper tea from Holland. Smuggling, along with earlier boycotts of British teas and other products over the past decade, had caused the British East India Company to suffer heavy financial losses, which necessitated the sale of their excess tea. King George thus lowered the price of British tea, so that even with the taxes it cost less than the smuggled alternatives; but the colonists still refused to buy British tea. When three

From John Hancock, "The Boston Massacre," delivered to the public in Boston, Massachusetts, March 5, 1774, as reprinted in *Early American Orations, 1760–1824*, edited by Louie R. Heller (New York: Macmillan, 1902).

British ships arrived in Boston harbor laden with tea chests, a group of Boston men dressed up as Native Americans boarded the ships and emptied their cargoes of tea into the Boston harbor—an act subsequently referred to as the Boston Tea Party.

In response, the British passed a series of acts known as the Coercive Acts against Boston and Massachusetts in early 1774. Aggressively reasserting its control, the Crown imported additional troops into Boston, dissolved the Massachusetts colonial charter, and closed Boston harbor to all trade until the city paid for the destroyed tea.

In the following speech, Hancock contrasts good government, which provides security and protection to its citizens, with tyranny. He also articulates his abhorrence of standing armies, differentiating between the positive role that armies can play in times of war and the "noxious vermin" of the British troops that fill Boston. Amidst this intolerable situation of tyranny, Hancock begins to call openly for American unity; to this end, he suggests a congress of representatives from each state who can work to unite the colonies and secure liberty and security for all Americans.

I have always, from my earliest youth, rejoiced in the felicity of my fellow-men; and have ever considered it as the indispensable duty of every member of society to promote, as far as in him lies, the prosperity of every individual, but more especially of the community to which he belongs; and also as a faithful subject of the State, to use his utmost endeavors to detect, and having detected, strenuously to oppose every traitorous plot which its enemies may devise for its destruction. Security to the persons and properties of the governed is so obviously the design and end of civil government, that to attempt a logical proof of it, would be like burning tapers at noonday to assist the sun in enlightening the world; and it cannot be either virtuous or honorable to attempt to support a government of which this is not the great and principal basis; and it is to the last degree vicious and infamous to attempt to support a government which manifestly tends to render the persons and properties of the governed insecure. Some boast of being friends to government; I am a friend to righteous government, to a government founded upon the principles of reason and justice; but I glory in publicly avowing my eternal enmity to tyranny. Is the present system, which the British administration have adopted for the government of the colonies, a righteous government, or is it tyranny? Here suffer me to ask (and would to Heaven there could be an answer) what tenderness, what regard, respect, or consideration has Great Britain shown, in their late transactions, for the security of the persons or properties of the inhabitants of the colonies? Or rather what have they omitted doing to destroy that security? They have declared that they have ever had, and of right ought ever to have, full power to make laws of sufficient validity to bind the colonies in all cases whatever. They have exercised this pretended right by imposing a tax on us without our consent; and lest we should show some reluctance at parting with our property, her fleets and armies are sent to enforce their mad pretensions. The town of Boston, ever faithful to the British Crown, has been invested by a British fleet: the troops of George III have crossed the wide Atlantic, not to engage an enemy, but to assist a band of traitors in trampling on the rights and liberties of his most loyal subjects in America— those rights and liberties which, as a father, he ought ever to regard, and as a King, he is bound, in honor, to defend from violation, even at the risk of his own life.

British Troops Abuse the People

Let not the history of the illustrious house of Brunswick inform posterity, that a King, descended from that glorious monarch, George II, once sent his British subjects to conquer and enslave his subjects in America. But be perpetual infamy entailed upon that villain who dared to advise his master to such execrable measures; for it was easy to foresee the consequences which so naturally followed upon sending troops into America, to enforce obedience to acts of the British Parliament, which neither God nor man ever empowered them to make. It was reasonable to expect that troops, who knew the errand they were sent upon, would treat the people whom they were to subjugate with a cruelty and haughtiness which too often buries the honorable character of a soldier in the disgraceful name of an unfeeling ruffian. The troops, upon their first arrival, took possession of our senate-house, and pointed their cannon against the judgment-hall, and even continued them there whilst the supreme court of judicature for this province was actually sitting there to decide upon the lives and fortunes of the King's subjects. Our streets nightly resounded with the noise of riot and debauchery, our peaceful citizens were hourly exposed to shameful insults, and often felt the effects of their violence and outrage. But this was not all: as though they thought it not enough to violate our civil rights, they endeavored to deprive us of the enjoyment of our religious privileges; to vitiate our morals, and thereby render us worthy of destruction. Hence the rude din of arms which broke in upon your solemn devotions in your temples, on that day hallowed by Heaven, and set apart by God himself for His peculiar worship. Hence, impious oaths and blasphemies so often tortured your unaccustomed ears. Hence, all the arts which idleness and luxury could invent were used to betray our youth of one sex into extravagance and effeminacy, and of the other, to infamy and ruin, and did they not succeed but too well? Did not a reverence for religion sensibly decay? Did not our infants almost learn to lisp out curses before they knew their horrid import? Did not our youth forget they were Americans, and regardless of the admonitions of the wise and aged servilely copy from their tyrants those vices which finally must overthrow the empire of Great Britain? And must I be compelled to acknowledge that even the noblest, fairest part of all the lower creation did not entirely escape the cursed snare? When virtue has once erected her throne in the female breast, it is upon so solid a basis that nothing is able to expel the heavenly inhabitant. But have there not been some, few indeed, I hope, whose youth and inexperience have rendered them a prey to wretches whom, upon the least reflection, they would have despised and hated as foes to God and their country? I fear there have been some such unhappy instances, or why have I seen an honest father clothed with shame; or why a virtuous mother drowned in tears?

The Boston Massacre

But I forbear, and come reluctantly to that dismal night when in such quick succession we felt the extremes of grief, astonishment, and rage; when Heaven in anger, for a dreadful moment, suffered hell to take the reins; when Satan with his chosen band opened the sluices of New England's blood, and sacrilegiously polluted our land with the dead bodies of her guiltless sons! Let this sad tale of death never be told without a tear; let not the heaving bosom cease to burn with manly indignation at the barbarous story, through the long tracts of future time: let every parent tell the shameful story to his listening children until tears of pity glisten in their eyes, and boiling passions shake their tender frames; and whilst the anniversary of that ill-fated night is kept a jubilee in the grim courts of pandemonium, let all America join in one common prayer to Heaven, that the inhuman, unprovoked murders of the fifth of March, 1770, planned by [Viscount Wills Hill] Hillsborough and a knot of treacherous knaves in Boston, and executed by the cruel hand of [Captain Thomas] Preston and his sanguinary coadjutors, may ever stand on history without a parallel. But what, my countrymen, withheld the ready arm of vengeance from executing instant justice on the vile assassins? Perhaps you feared promiscuous carnage might ensue, and that the innocent might share the fate of those who had performed the infernal deed? But were not all guilty? Were you not too tender of the lives of those who came to fix a yoke on your necks? But I must not too severely blame a fault which great souls only can commit. May that magnificence of spirit which scorns the low pursuit of malice, may that generous compassion which often preserves from ruin, even a guilty villain, forever actuate the noble bosoms of Americans! But let not the miscreant host vainly imagine that we feared their arms. No; them we despised; we dread nothing but slavery. Death is the creature of a poltroon's brains; 'tis immortality to sacrifice ourselves for the salvation of our country. We fear not death. That gloomy night, the pale-faced moon, and the affrighted stars that hurried through the sky, can witness that we fear not death. Our hearts which, at the recollection, glow with rage that four revolving years have scarcely taught us to restrain, can witness that we fear not death; and happy it is for those who dared to insult us, that their naked bodies are not now piled up, an everlasting monument to Massachusetts' bravery. But they retired, they fled, and in that flight they found their only safety. We then expected that the hand of public justice would soon inflict that punishment upon the murderers, which by the laws of God and man they had incurred. But let the unbiased pen of a [British journalist James] Robertson, or perhaps of some equally famed American, conduct this trial before the great tribunal of succeeding generations. And though the murderers may escape the just resentment of an outraged people; though drowsy justice, intoxicated by the poisonous draught prepared for her cup still nods upon her rotten seat, yet be assured such complicated crimes will meet their due reward. . . .

Britain Is Trying to Enslave Us

True it is, that the British ministry have annexed a salary to the office of the governor of this province, to be paid out of a revenue raised in America, without our consent. They have attempted to render our courts of justice the instruments of extending the authority of acts of the British Parliament over this colony, by making the judges dependent on the British administration for their support. But this people will never be enslaved with their eyes open. The moment they knew that the governor was not such a governor as the charter of the province points out, he lost his power of hurting them. They were alarmed; they suspected him—have guarded against him, and he has found that a wise and a brave people, when they know their danger, are fruitful in expedients to escape it.

The courts of judicature, also, so far lost their dignity, by being supposed to be under an undue influence, that our representatives thought it absolutely necessary to resolve that they were bound to declare, that they would not receive any

Many residents of Boston viewed the British Crown's reaction to the Boston Tea Party as overreaching and tyrannical.

other salary besides that which the general court should grant them; and if they did not make this declaration, that it would be the duty of the House to impeach them.

Great expectations were also formed from the artful scheme of allowing the East India Company to export tea to America upon their own account. This certainly, had it succeeded, would have effected the purpose of the contrivers, and gratified the most sanguine wishes of our adversaries. We soon should have found our trade in the hands of foreigners, and taxes imposed on everything we consumed; nor would it have been strange, if, in a few years, a company in London should have purchased an exclusive right of trading to America. But their plot was soon discovered. The people soon were aware of the poison which, with so much craft and subtility, had been concealed. Loss and disgrace ensued; and perhaps this long-concerted masterpiece of policy may issue in the total disuse of tea in this country, which will eventually be the saving of the lives and the estates of thousands. Yet, while we rejoice that the adversary has not hitherto prevailed against us, let us by no means put off the harness. Restless malice and disappointed ambition will still suggest new measures to our inveterate enemies. Therefore, let us also be ready to take the field whenever danger calls; let us be united and strengthen the hands of each other by promoting a general union among us. Much has been done by the committees of correspondence, for this and the other towns of this province, toward uniting the inhabitants; let them still go on and prosper. Much has been done by the committees of correspondence for the Houses of Assembly, in this and our sister colonies, for uniting the inhabitants of the whole continent, for the security of their common interest. May success ever attend their generous endeavors. But permit me here to suggest a general congress of deputies, from the several Houses of Assembly on the continent, as the most effectual method of establishing such a union as the present posture of our affairs requires. At such a congress, a firm foundation may be laid for the security of our rights and liberties; a system may be formed for our common safety, by a strict adherence to which we shall be able to frustrate any attempt to overthrow our constitution; restore peace and harmony to America, and secure honor and wealth to Great Britain, even against the inclinations of her ministers, whose duty it is to study her welfare; and we shall also free ourselves from those unmannerly pillagers who impudently tell us, that they are licensed by an act of the British Parliament to thrust their dirty hands into the pockets of every American. But I trust the happy time will come, when, with the besom of destruction, those noxious vermin will be swept forever from the streets of Boston.

Break the Bonds

Surely you never will tamely suffer this country to be a den of thieves. Remember, my friends, from whom you sprang. Let not a meanness of spirit, unknown to those whom you boast of as your fathers, excite a thought to the dishonor of your mothers. I conjure you, by all that is dear, by all that is honorable, by all that is sacred, not only that ye pray, but that ye act; that, if necessary, ye fight, and even die, for the prosperity of our Jerusalem. Break in sunder, with noble disdain, the bonds with which the Philistines have bound you. Suffer not yourselves to be betrayed, by the soft arts of luxury and effeminacy, into the pit digged for your destruction. Despise the glare of wealth. That people who pay greater respect to a wealthy villain than to an honest, upright man in poverty almost deserve to be enslaved; they plainly show that wealth, however it may be acquired, is, in their esteem, to be preferred to virtue.

But I thank God that America abounds in men who are superior to all temptation, whom nothing can divert from a steady pursuit of the interest of their country, who are at once its ornament and its safeguard. And sure I am, I should not incur your displeasure, if I paid a respect, so justly due to their much honored characters, in this place. But when I name an Adams, such a numerous host of fellow-patriots rush upon my mind that I fear it would take up too much of your time should I attempt to call over the illustrious roll. But your grateful hearts will point you to the men; and their revered names, in all succeeding times, shall grace the annals of America. From them let us, my friends, take example; from them let us catch the divine enthusiasm; and feel, each for himself, the godlike pleasure of diffusing happiness on all around us; of delivering the oppressed from the iron grasp of tyranny; of changing the hoarse complaints and bitter moans of wretched slaves into those cheerful songs which freedom and contentment must inspire. There is a heartfelt satisfaction in reflecting on our exertions for the public weal, which all the sufferings an enraged tyrant can inflict will never take away; which the ingratitude and reproaches of those whom we have saved from ruin, cannot rob us of. The virtuous asserter of the rights of mankind merits a reward, which even a want of success in his endeavors to save his country, the heaviest misfortune which can befall a genuine patriot, cannot entirely prevent him from receiving.

I have the most animating confidence that the present noble struggle for liberty will terminate gloriously for America. And let us play the man for our God, and for the cities of our God; while we are using the means in our power, let us humbly commit our righteous cause to the great Lord of the universe, who loveth righteousness and hateth iniquity. And having secured the approbation of our hearts, by a faithful and unwearied discharge of our duty to our country, let us joyfully leave our concerns in the hands of Him who raiseth up and pulleth down the empires and kingdoms of the world as He pleases;

and with cheerful submission to His sovereign will, devoutly say, "Although the fig-tree shall not blossom, neither shall fruit be in the vines; the labor of the olive shall fail, and the field shall yield no meat; the flock shall be cut off from the fold, and there shall be no herd in the stalls; yet we will rejoice in the Lord, we will joy in the God of our salvation."

The British Should Reconcile with the Colonies

Edmund Burke

In the fall of 1774, the British army seized the arms and ammunition that the American colonists had stored near Boston; in response, citizens organized the "minute-men," groups of armed men who would be ready at a minute's notice if need be. The British troops waited in Boston throughout the fall and winter of 1774, while back in England, the debate about the rebellious colonies raged furiously, with the city of Boston pinpointed as the focal point for the wrath of the entire British Empire.

In North America, colonists were split into two camps. While some Americans, called "Loyalists," still felt strong ties to Britain, others were making military preparations to fight for their freedom from British rule. Similarly, the British Parliament was split. William Pitt and the supporters of America advocated withdrawing troops from Boston in an effort to avert violence and re-sume the profitable commercial relationship with the American colonies. A larger contingent, including King George, had decided that it was time for war: Some felt that the great British Empire needed to assert its military power over the "rebels," as the American patriots were called; others simply believed that after years of escalat-ing tensions, armed conflict was unavoidable.

Edmund Burke, a noted political philosopher and member of the British Parliament who had served as sec-retary to Lord Rockingham for many years, was an ar-

From Edmund Burke, "Conciliation with the Colonies," address to the House of Commons, London, England, March 22, 1775, as reprinted in *Orations and Ar-guments by English and American Statesmen*, edited by Cornelius Beach Bradley (Boston: Allyn & Bacon, 1895).

dent supporter of American liberty. During the crisis following the unrest in America, he remained a staunch supporter of peace and total conciliation with the colonies,
and he took on most of the British Parliament to argue
for it. Knowing that Parliament would not be persuaded
by abstract arguments about rights, Burke pragmatically
suggested that peace was in the best interests of Britain
and was the most logical solution. In the following excerpts from a speech delivered to the House of Commons
on March 22, 1775, he argues eloquently that the withdrawal of British troops, the cessation of taxes, the
restoration of self-government, and full reconciliation
with the American colonies is Britain's most politically
shrewd and economically longsighted approach.

The proposition is peace. Not peace through the
medium of war; not peace to be hunted through the
labyrinth of intricate and endless negotiations; not
peace to arise out of universal discord fomented, from principle, in all parts of the Empire; not peace to depend on the
juridical determination of perplexing questions, or the pre-
cise marking the shadowy boundaries of a complex government. It is simple peace; sought in its natural course, and in
its ordinary haunts. It is peace sought in the spirit of peace,
and laid in principles purely pacific. I propose, by removing
the ground of the difference, and by restoring the former un-
suspecting confidence of the Colonies in the Mother Country, to give permanent satisfaction to your people; and (far
from a scheme of ruling by discord) to reconcile them to each
other in the same act and by the bond of the very same interest which reconciles them to British government. . . .

I mean to give peace. Peace implies reconciliation; and
where there has been a material dispute, reconciliation does
in a manner always imply concession on the one part or on
the other. In this state of things I make no difficulty in af-
firming that the proposal ought to originate, from us. Great
and acknowledged force is not impaired, either in effect or in
opinion, by an unwillingness to exert itself. The superior

power may offer peace with honor and with safety. Such an offer from such a power will be attributed to magnanimity. But the concessions of the weak are the concessions of fear. When such a one is disarmed, he is wholly at the mercy of his superior; and he loses forever that time and those chances, which, as they happen to all men, are the strength and resources of all inferior power.

The capital leading questions on which you must this day decide are these two: First, whether you ought to concede; and secondly, what your concession ought to be. On the first of these questions we have gained . . . some ground. But I am sensible that a good deal more is still to be done. . . .

Force Will Not Secure Victory

America, gentlemen say, is a noble object. It is an object well worth fighting for. Certainly it is, if fighting a people be the best way of gaining them. Gentlemen in this respect will be led to their choice of means by their complexions and their habits. Those who understand the military art will of course have some predilection for it. Those who wield the thunder of the state may have more confidence in the efficacy of arms. But I confess, possibly for want of this knowledge, my opinion is much more in favor of prudent management than of force; considering force not as an odious, but a feeble instrument for preserving a people so numerous, so active, so growing, so spirited as this, in a profitable and subordinate connection with us.

First, Sir, permit me to observe that the use of force alone is but temporary. It may subdue for a moment, but it does not remove the necessity of subduing again; and a nation is not governed which is perpetually to be conquered.

My next objection is its uncertainty. Terror is not always the effect of force, and an armament is not a victory. If you do not succeed, you are without resource; for, conciliation failing, force remains; but, force failing, no further hope of reconciliation is left. Power and authority are sometimes bought by kindness; but they can never be begged as alms by an impoverished and defeated violence.

A further objection to force is, that you impair the object

by your very endeavors to preserve it. The thing you fought for is not the thing which you recover; but depreciated, sunk, wasted, and consumed in the contest. Nothing less will content me than *whole America*. I do not choose to consume its strength along with our own, because in all parts it is the British strength that I consume. I do not choose to be caught by a foreign enemy at the end of this exhausting conflict; and still less in the midst of it. I may escape; but I can make no insurance against such an event. Let me add, that I do not choose wholly to break the American spirit; because it is the spirit that has made the country.

Lastly, we have no sort of experience in favor of force as an instrument in the rule of our Colonies. Their growth and their utility has been owing to methods altogether different. Our ancient indulgence has been said to be pursued to a fault. It may be so. But we know, if feeling is evidence, that our fault was more tolerable than our attempt to mend it; and our sin far more salutary than our penitence.

These, Sir, are my reasons for not entertaining that high opinion of untried force by which many gentlemen, for whose sentiments in other particulars I have great respect, seem to be so greatly captivated. But there is still behind a third consideration concerning this object which serves to determine my opinion on the sort of policy which ought to be pursued in the management of America . . . I mean its temper and character.

In this character of the Americans, a love of freedom is the predominating feature which marks and distinguishes the whole; and as an ardent is always a jealous affection, your Colonies become suspicious, restive, and untractable whenever they see the least attempt to wrest from them by force, or shuffle from them by chicane, what they think the only advantage worth living for. This fierce spirit of liberty is stronger in the English Colonies probably than in any other people of the earth, and this from a great variety of powerful causes; which, to understand the true temper of their minds and the direction which this spirit takes, it will not be amiss to lay open somewhat more largely.

First, the people of the Colonies are descendants of Englishmen. England, Sir, is a nation which still, I hope, respects, and formerly adored, her freedom. The Colonists emigrated

from you when this part of your character was most pre-
dominant; and they took this bias and direction the moment
they parted from your hands. They are therefore not only devoted to liberty, but to liberty according to English ideas, and
on English principles. Abstract liberty, like other mere ab-
stractions, is not to be found. Liberty inheres in some sensible object; and every nation has formed to itself some favorite point, which by way of eminence becomes the criterion
of their happiness. It happened, you know, Sir, that the great
contests for freedom in this country were from the earliest
times chiefly upon the question of taxing. Most of the contests in the ancient commonwealths turned primarily on the
right of election of magistrates; or on the balance among the
several orders of the state. The question of money was not
with them so immediate. But in England it was otherwise.
On this point of taxes the ablest pens, and most eloquent
tongues, have been exercised; the greatest spirits have acted
and suffered. In order to give the fullest satisfaction concerning the importance of this point, it was not only necessary for
those who in argument defended the excellence of the English
Constitution to insist on this privilege of granting money as
a dry point of fact, and to prove that the right had been acknowledged in ancient parchments and blind usages to reside
in a certain body called a House of Commons. They went
much farther; they attempted to prove, and they succeeded,
that in theory it ought to be so, from the particular nature of
a House of Commons as an immediate representative of the
people, whether the old records had delivered this oracle or
not. They took infinite pains to inculcate, as a fundamental
principle, that in all monarchies the people must in effect
themselves, mediately or immediately, possess the power of
granting their own money, or no shadow of liberty can subsist. The Colonies draw from you, as with their life-blood,
these ideas and principles. Their love of liberty, as with you,
fixed and attached on this specific point of taxing. Liberty
might be safe, or might be endangered, in twenty other particulars, without their being much pleased or alarmed. Here
they felt its pulse; and as they found that beat, they thought
themselves sick or sound. I do not say whether they were
right or wrong in applying your general arguments to their

own case. It is not easy, indeed, to make a monopoly of theorems and corollaries. The fact is, that they did thus apply those general arguments; and your mode of governing them, whether through lenity or indolence, through wisdom or mistake, confirmed them in the imagination that they, as well as you, had an interest in these common principles.

They were further confirmed in this pleasing error by the form of their provincial legislative assemblies. Their governments are popular in an high degree; some are merely popular; in all, the popular representative is the most weighty; and this share of the people in their ordinary government never fails to inspire them with lofty sentiments, and with a strong aversion from whatever tends to deprive them of their chief importance.

If anything were wanting to this necessary operation of the form of government, religion would have given it a complete effect. Religion, always a principle of energy, in this new people is no way worn out or impaired; and their mode of professing it is also one main cause of this free spirit. The people are Protestants; and of that kind which is the most adverse to all implicit submission of mind and opinion. This is a persuasion not only favorable to liberty, but built upon it. . . .

An Abundance of Lawyers

Permit me, Sir, to add another circumstance in our Colonies which contributes no mean part towards the growth and effect of this untractable spirit. I mean their education. In no country perhaps in the world is the law so general a study. The profession itself is numerous and powerful; and in most provinces it takes the lead. The greater number of the deputies sent to the Congress were lawyers. But all who read, and most do read, endeavor to obtain some smattering in that science. I have been told by an eminent bookseller, that in no branch of his business, after tracts of popular devotion, were so many books as those on the law exported to the Plantations. The Colonists have now fallen into the way of printing them for their own use. I hear that they have sold nearly as many of [British jurist Sir William] Blackstone's Commentaries [on the Laws of England] in America as in England. General [Thomas] Gage marks out this disposition very particularly in a letter on your table. He states that all the people in his government are lawyers, or smatterers in law; and that in Boston they have been enabled, by successful chicane, wholly to evade many parts of one of your capital penal constitutions. The smartness of debate will say that this knowledge ought to teach them more clearly the rights of legislature, their obligations to obedience, and the penalties of rebellion. All this is mighty well. But my honorable and learned friend on the floor, who condescends to mark what I say for animadversion, will disdain that ground. He has heard, as well as I, that when great honors and great emoluments do not win over this knowledge to the service of the state, it is a formidable adversary to government. If the spirit be not tamed and broken by these happy methods, it is stubborn and litigious. *Abeunt studia in mores.* This study renders men acute, inquisitive, dexterous, prompt in attack, ready in defence, full of resources. In other countries, the people, more simple, and of a less mercurial cast, judge of an ill principle in government only by an actual grievance; here they anticipate the evil, and judge of the pressure of the grievance by the badness of the principle. They augur misgovernment at a distance, and snuff the approach of tyranny in every tainted breeze.

The last cause of this disobedient spirit in the Colonies is hardly less powerful than the rest, as it is not merely moral, but laid deep in the natural constitution of things. Three thousand miles of ocean lie between you and them. No contrivance can prevent the effect of this distance in weakening government. Seas roll, and months pass, between the order and the execution; and the want of a speedy explanation of a single point is enough to defeat a whole system. You have, indeed, winged ministers of vengeance, who carry your bolts in their pounces to the remotest verge of the sea. But there a power steps in that limits the arrogance of raging passions and furious elements, and says, *So far shalt thou go, and no farther.* Who are you, that you should fret and rage, and bite the chains of nature? Nothing worse happens to you than does to all nations who have extensive empire; and it happens in all the forms into which empire can be thrown. In large bodies the circulation of power must be less vigorous at the extremities. . . .

The Spirit of Liberty

From all these causes a fierce spirit of liberty has grown up. It has grown with the growth of the people in your Colonies, and increased with the increase of their wealth; a spirit that unhappily meeting with an exercise of power in England which, however lawful, is not reconcilable to any ideas of liberty, much less with theirs, has kindled this flame that is ready to consume us.

Liberty or Death

Patrick Henry

While Edmund Burke was vainly attempting to persuade the British Parliament to pursue a course of reconciliation, on the other side of the Atlantic and on the very next day, Virginia statesman Patrick Henry was declaring that the time for speeches was over and that now was the time for war. Henry was known to be far more militant than many of his contemporaries, and as he spoke before the Virginia legislature urging military preparedness, many of his peers were of mixed feelings.

Throughout the tense months of winter, the leaders of all the state legislatures had been debating their next steps while waiting to hear from King George and hoping that reconciliation was still possible. Henry, however, had long been of the opinion that an armed confrontation was unavoidable. Here, he berates his countrymen for holding foolish hopes of peace, exclaiming: "Gentlemen may cry, Peace, peace—but there is no peace. The war is actually begun!" A mere month before the battles of Concord and Lexington, his words were indeed prophetic.

Unfortunately, Henry's speech was not recorded or published in his time. The version that follows is what Henry's biographer, William Wirt, reconstructed from people who had heard the speech twenty-five years earlier. While one can be certain that the exact wording is not identical, the sentiments expressed reflects the views of this important leader.

From Patrick Henry, "Liberty or Death," addressed to the Second Revolutionary Convention of Virginia, Richmond, Virginia, March 23, 1775, as reprinted in *Select Orations Illustrating American Political History*, edited by Samuel Bannister Harding (New York: Macmillan, 1909).

Mr. President: No man thinks more highly than I do of the patriotism, as well as abilities, of the very worthy gentlemen who have just addressed the house. But different men often see the same subject in different lights; and, therefore, I hope it will not be thought disrespectful to those gentlemen if, entertaining as I do opinions of a character very opposite to theirs, I shall speak forth my sentiments freely and without reserve. This is no time for ceremony. The question before the house is one of awful moment to this country. For my own part, I consider it as nothing less than a question of freedom or slavery; and in proportion to the magnitude of the subject ought to be the freedom of the debate. It is only in this way that we can hope to arrive at truth, and fulfil the great responsibility which we hold to God and our country. Should I keep back my opinions at such a time through fear of giving offense, I should consider myself as guilty of treason towards my country, and of an act of disloyalty toward the Majesty of Heaven which I revere above all earthly kings.

The Time for Hope Is Over

Mr. President, it is natural to man to indulge in the illusions of hope. We are apt to shut our eyes against a painful truth, and listen to the song of that siren till she transforms us into beasts. Is this the part of wise men engaged in a great and arduous struggle for liberty? Are we disposed to be of the number of those who having eyes see not, and having ears hear not, the things which so nearly concern their temporal salvation? For my part, whatever anguish of spirit it may cost, I am willing to know the whole truth; to know the worst and to provide for it.

I have but one lamp by which my feet are guided; and that is the lamp of experience. I know of no way of judging of the future but by the past. And judging by the past, I wish to know what there has been in the conduct of the British ministry for the last ten years to justify those hopes with which gentlemen have been pleased to solace themselves and the house? Is it that insidious smile with which our petition has been lately received? Trust it not, sir; it will prove a snare to your feet. Suffer not yourselves to be betrayed with a kiss. Ask yourselves how this gracious reception of our petition comports with those warlike preparations which cover our waters and darken our land. Are fleets and armies necessary to a work of love and reconciliation? Have we shown ourselves so unwilling to be reconciled that force must be called in to win back our love? Let us not deceive ourselves, sir. These are the implements of war and subjugation; the last arguments to which kings resort. I ask gentlemen, sir, what means this martial array, if its purpose be not to force us to submission? Can gentlemen assign any other possible motive for it? Has Great Britain any enemy in this quarter of the world to call for all this accumulation of navies and armies? No, sir, she has none. They are meant for us; they can be meant for no other. They are sent over to bind and rivet upon us those chains which the British ministry have been so long forging. And what have we to oppose to them? Shall we try argument? Sir, we have been trying that for the last ten years. Have we anything new to offer upon the subject? Nothing. We have held the subject up in every light of which it is capable; but it has been all in vain. Shall we resort to entreaty and humble supplication? What terms shall we find which have not been already exhausted?

Let us not, I beseech you, sir, deceive ourselves longer. Sir, we have done everything that could be done to avert the storm which is now coming on. We have petitioned; we have remonstrated; we have supplicated; we have prostrated ourselves before the throne, and have implored its interposition to arrest the tyrannical hands of the ministry and Parliament. Our petitions have been slighted; our remonstrances have produced additional violence and insult; our supplications have been disregarded; and we have been spurned with contempt from the foot of the throne. In vain, after these things, may we indulge in the fond hope of peace and reconciliation. There is no longer any room for hope. If we wish to be free—if we mean to preserve inviolate those inestimable privileges for which we have been so long contending—if we mean not basely to abandon the noble struggle in which we have been so long engaged, and which we have pledged ourselves never to abandon until the glorious object of our contest shall be obtained—we must fight! I repeat it, sir, we must fight! An appeal to arms and to the God of Hosts is all that is left us!

We Must Arm Ourselves Immediately

They tell us, sir, that we are weak, unable to cope with so formidable an adversary. But when shall we be stronger? Will it be the next week, or the next year? Will it be when we are totally disarmed, and when a British guard shall be stationed in every house? Shall we gather strength by irresolution and inaction? Shall we acquire the means of effectual resistance by lying supinely on our backs and hugging the delusive phantom of hope until our enemies shall have bound us hand and foot? Sir, we are not weak if we make a proper use of those means which the God of nature hath placed in our power. Three millions of people, armed in the holy cause of liberty, and in such a country as that which we possess, are invincible by any force which our enemy can send against us. Besides, sir, we shall not fight our battles alone. There is a just God who presides over the destinies of nations, and who will raise up friends to fight our battles for us. The battle, sir, is not to the strong alone; it is to the vigilant, the active, the brave. Besides, sir, we have no election. If we were base enough to desire it, it is now too late to retire from the contest. There is no retreat but in submission and slavery! Our chains are forged! Their clinking may be heard on the plains of Boston! The war is inevitable—and let it come! I repeat it, sir, let it come.

It is in vain, sir, to extenuate the matter. Gentlemen may cry, Peace, peace!—but there is no peace. The war is actually begun! The next gale that sweeps from the north will bring to our ears the clash of resounding arms! Our brethren are already in the field! Why stand we here idle? What is it that gentlemen wish? What would they have? Is life so dear, or peace so sweet, as to be purchased at the price of chains and slavery? Forbid it, Almighty God! I know not what course others may take; but as for me, *give me liberty, or give me death!*

CHAPTER

TWO

Fundamental Principles of Democracy: Liberty and Free Speech

Natural Versus Civil Liberty

John Winthrop

Although there were earlier French and Spanish settlements, the Puritans are considered the founders of America because their ideas and beliefs were fundamental in shaping New England society in the seventeenth century and forming the bedrock of American culture. The Puritans had left England as a result of their strong religious differences with the Church of England: They wished to "purify" the church of what they perceived to be popish practices and internal corruption. After decades of religious persecution and failed attempts at reforming the church from within, the Puritans fled to Holland, where they lived for about ten years. In danger of losing their English language and culture, however, they set off to establish their religion-based society in the New World.

In 1628, the Puritans attained a charter for Massachusetts Bay, which gave them the right to set up a government, and within two years, four ships set sail for North America. John Winthrop, who had been chosen as the new governor, arrived on the first ship, the *Arabella*, with a vision of Massachusetts as a refuge from the Antichrist (as King Charles I was referred to). For Winthrop, the author of the following speech, Massachusetts was to be the new Jerusalem: a place steeped in religion, where civil law was to be based on the Bible, and lawmakers were viewed as God's assistants on earth.

Yet although the Puritans were themselves seeking religious asylum, they were notably intolerant of others who held different beliefs. Winthrop banished both Anne

From John Winthrop, "On Liberty," delivered in Massachusetts, 1645, as reprinted in *American Voices: Significant Speeches in American History, 1640–1945*, edited by James Andrews and David Zarefsky (New York: Longman, 1989).

Hutchinson and Roger Williams for challenging his views about the religious authority vested in civic officials and for espousing divergent interpretations of Christian ideologies. For the Puritans, there was but one way to worship God—*their* way—and they felt justified in persecuting all those who disagreed with them in the name of "God's truth." Hutchinson started a new settlement in Cape Cod, while Williams established Providence, Rhode Island, which was perceived as a "Sodom" of liberal sin and debauchery for several decades.

Although Winthrop despised democracy, was highly intolerant, and viewed government as a religious institution, he did believe that the public good should always take precedence over private interests, and this forms the basis of his notion of social justice. The following speech was delivered to a Massachusetts crowd in 1645 after Winthrop was impeached for his unpopular choice in selecting a militia captain. (He was subsequently pardoned and continued to govern for many years.) In his description of his political views, Winthrop reviles "natural" liberty as being corrupt and opposed to authority. He praises what he calls "civil" liberty, which is the social organization grounded in "the covenant between God and man."

I suppose something may be expected from me upon this charge that has befallen me, which moves me to speak now to you; yet I intend not to intermeddle in the proceedings of the court or with any of the persons concerned therein. Only I bless God that I see an issue of this troublesome business. I also acknowledge the justice of the court, and for mine own part I am well satisfied. I was publicly charged, and I am publicly and legally acquitted, which is all I did expect or desire. And though this be sufficient for my justification before men, yet not so before the God who hath seen so much amiss in my dispensations (and even in this affair) as calls me to be humble.

For to be publicly and criminally charged in this court is

matter of humiliation (and I desire to make a right use of it), notwithstanding I be thus acquitted. If her father had spit in her face (saith the Lord concerning Miriam), should she not have been ashamed seven days? Shame had lien upon her, whatever the occasion had been. I am unwilling to stay you from your urgent affairs, yet give me leave (upon this special occasion) to speak a little more to this assembly. It may be of some good use to inform and rectify the judgments of some of the people, and may prevent such distempers as have arisen amongst us.

Magistrates

The great questions that have troubled the country are about the authority of the magistrates and the liberty of the people. It is yourselves who have called us to this office, and, being called by you, we have our authority from God, in way of an ordinance, such as hath the image of God eminently stamped upon it, the contempt and violation whereof hath been vindicated with examples of divine vengeance.

I entreat you to consider that, when you choose magistrates, you take them from among yourselves, men subject to like passions as you are. Therefore, when you see infirmities in us, you should reflect upon your own, and that would make you bear the more with us, and not be severe censurers of the failings of your magistrates, when you have continual experience of the like infirmities in yourselves and others.

We account him a good servant who breaks not his covenant. The covenant between you and us is the oath you have taken of us, which is to this purpose, that we shall govern you and judge your causes by the rules of God's laws and our own, according to our best skill. When you agree with a workman to build you a ship or house, etc., he undertakes as well for his skill as for his faithfulness; for it is his profession, and you pay him for both. But when you call one to be a magistrate he doth not profess or undertake to have sufficient skill for that office, nor can you furnish him with gifts, etc., therefore you must run the hazard of his skill and ability. But if he fail in faithfulness, which by his oath he is bound unto, that he must answer for. If it fall out that the case be clear to common apprehension, and the rule clear also, if he transgress here, the error is not in the skill, but in the evil of the will: it must be required of him. But if the case be doubtful, or the rule doubtful, to men of such understanding and parts as your magistrates are, if your magistrates should err here, yourselves must bear it.

Natural Liberty

For the other point concerning liberty, I observe a great mistake in the country about that. There is a twofold liberty, natural (I mean as our nature is now corrupt) and civil or federal. The first is common to man with beasts and other creatures. By this man, as he stands in relation to man simply, hath liberty to do what he lists: it is a liberty to evil as well as to good. This liberty is incompatible and inconsistent with authority, and cannot endure the least restraint of the most just authority. The exercise and maintaining of this liberty makes men grow more evil, and in time to be worse than brute beasts: *omnes sumus licentia deteriores* [all men deteriorate with freedom]. This is that great enemy of truth and peace, that wild beast, which all the ordinances of God are bent against, to restrain and subdue it.

Civil Liberty

The other kind of liberty I call civil or federal; it may also be termed moral, in reference to the covenant between God and man in the moral law, and the politic covenants and constitutions amongst men themselves. This liberty is the proper end and object of authority, and cannot subsist without it; and it is a liberty to that only which is good, just, and honest. This liberty you are to stand for, with the hazard (not only of your goods, but) of your lives, if need be. Whatsoever crosseth this is not authority, but a distemper thereof. This liberty is maintained and exercised in a way of subjection to authority; it is of the same kind of liberty wherewith Christ hath made us free. The woman's own choice makes such a man her husband; yet, being so chosen, he is her lord, and she is to be subject to him, yet in a way of liberty, not of bondage; and a true wife accounts her subjection her honor and freedom, and would not think her condition safe and free but in her subjection to her husband's authority. Such is the liberty of the church under the authority of Christ, her king and husband; his yoke is so easy and sweet to her as a bride's ornaments; and if, through forwardness or wantonness, etc., she shake it off at any time, she is at no rest in her spirit until she take it up again; and whether her lord smiles upon her, and embraceth her in his arms, or whether he frowns, or rebukes, or smites her, she apprehends the sweetness of his love in all, and is refreshed, supported, and instructed by every such dispensation of his authority over her. On the other side, ye know who they are that complain of this yoke and say, let us break their bands, etc., we will not have this man to rule over us.

Even so, brethren, it will be between you and your magistrates. If you stand for your natural corrupt liberties, and will do what is good in your own eyes, you will not endure the least weight of authority, but will murmur, and oppose, and be always striving to shake off that yoke; but if you will be satisfied to enjoy such civil and lawful liberties, such as Christ allows you, then will you quietly and cheerfully submit unto that authority which is set over you, in all the administrations of it, for your good. Wherein, if we fail at any time, we hope we shall be willing (by God's assistance) to hearken to good advice from any of you, or in any other way to God; so shall your liberties be preserved, in upholding the honor and power of authority amongst you.

An Argument for Freedom of the Press

Andrew Hamilton

During the eighteenth century, newspapers became an increasingly important forum for public debate and the expression of opinion. Newspapers were integrally connected to other forms of expression such as oratory; often speeches would be reprinted and widely circulated in newspapers, and the contents of a local speech could thus circulate throughout the colonies. Yet for the first few decades of the eighteenth century, editors were fearful about expressing their true opinions, for they were frequently thrown in jail when they did. James Franklin, for example, Benjamin Franklin's brother and the editor of the *New England Courant*, was jailed in the 1720s for printing views that criticized the authorities.

In New York in 1733, another printer, a German immigrant by the name of John Peter Zenger, criticized the corrupt New York administration and was arrested. The royally appointed governor, William Cosby, had made himself extremely unpopular through his arrogant and intolerant measures, one of which included removing the chief justice of New York from a case in favor of a more partial judge. While one of the main newspapers in New York at that time, the *New York Gazette*, became the mouthpiece for the governor's office, Zenger published a series of anonymous critiques of the governor in the *New York Weekly Journal*. Although Zenger himself did not author the writings, he was considered to be legally re-

---

From Andrew Hamilton's speech in defense of John Peter Zenger, August 4, 1735, as reprinted in *The World's Best Orations*, edited by David J. Brewer (Chicago: Ferd. P. Kaiser, 1923).

sponsible for printing them. At the governor's orders, his press was burned and he was arrested.

Although Zenger was acquitted by a jury of his peers, Governor Cosby overturned the verdict and recharged him with seditious libel. When Zenger's attorneys queried the jurisdiction of the governor, they were effectively disbarred in New York. Lacking legal counsel, Zenger remained in jail for ten months until one of the most respected attorneys in the colonies—Andrew Hamilton—came to his rescue.

Hamilton, former attorney general of Pennsylvania and the speaker for the General Assembly, was not only outraged at the abject state of corruption into which the New York government had descended, but he was also concerned about the possibility that such tyranny could spread to other states if allowed to continue unchecked. In the following excerpts from his speech at the trial, Hamilton essentially argues that if a statement is true, it cannot be considered libelous. He thus asks the jury to decide not only whether Zenger was guilty of printing the material, but also whether they consider his words to be libelous or "the just complaints of a number of men, who suffer under a bad administration."

Hamilton won the case, Zenger was freed, and the colonists won the right to freedom of expression. Zenger returned to the printing business—and so did others; by 1760 there were more than twenty newspapers throughout the colonies. This landmark case thus stimulated the growth of print media and encouraged communication and the spread of opinion in the decades preceding the American Revolution.

May it please your honors, I agree with Mr. Attorney [opposing counsel and Attorney-General of New York, Richard Bradley] that government is a sacred thing, but I differ very widely from him when he would insinuate that the just complaints of a number of men, who suffer under a bad administration, is libeling that administration. Had I believed that to be law, I should not have given the court the trouble of hearing anything that I could say in this cause. I own when I read the information, I had not the art to find out (without the help of Mr. Attorney's innuendos) that the Governor was the person meant in every period of that newspaper; and I was inclined to believe that they were written by some, who, from an extraordinary zeal for liberty, had misconstrued the conduct of some persons in authority into crimes; and that Mr. Attorney, out of his too great zeal for power, had exhibited this information to correct the indiscretion of my client, and at the same time to show his superiors the great concern he had, lest they should be treated with any undue freedom. But from what Mr. Attorney has just now said, to wit, that this prosecution was directed by the Governor and council, and from the extraordinary appearance of people of all conditions which I observe in court upon this occasion, I have reason to think that those in the administration have by this prosecution something more in view, and that the people believe they have a good deal more at stake than I apprehended; and therefore, as it is become my duty to be both plain and particular in this cause, I beg leave to bespeak the patience of the court. . . .

There is heresy in law as well as in religion, and both have changed very much; and we well know that it is not two centuries ago that a man would have been burned as a heretic for owning such opinions in matters of religion as are publicly written and printed at this day. They were fallible men, it seems, and we take the liberty, not only to differ from them in religious opinion, but to condemn them and their opinions too; and I must presume that in taking these freedoms in thinking and speaking about matters of faith or religion, we are in the right; for, though it is said there are very great liberties of this kind taken in New York, yet I have heard of no information preferred by Mr. Attorney for any offenses of this sort. From which I think it is pretty clear that in New York a man may make very free with his God, but he must take special care what he says of his Governor. It is agreed upon by all men that this is a reign of liberty, and while men keep within the bounds of truth, I hope they may with safety both speak and write their sentiments of the conduct of men of power; I mean of that part of their conduct only which affects the liberty or property of the people under their administration; were this to be denied, then the next step may make them slaves. For what notions can be entertained of slavery, beyond that of suffering the greatest injuries and oppressions, without the liberty of complaining; or if they do, to be destroyed, body and estate, for so doing?

Abuse of Power

It is said, and insisted upon by Mr. Attorney, that government is a sacred thing; that it is to be supported and reverenced; it is government that protects our persons and estates; that prevents treasons, murders, robberies, riots, and all the train of evils that overturn kingdoms and states, and ruin particular persons; and if those in the administration, especially the supreme magistrates, must have all their conduct censured by private men, government cannot subsist. This is called a licentiousness not to be tolerated. It is said that it brings the rulers of the people into contempt so that their authority is not regarded, and so that in the end the laws cannot be put in execution. These, I say, and such as these, are the general topics insisted upon by men in power and their advocates. But I wish it might be considered at the same time how often it has happened that the abuse of power has been the primary cause of these evils, and that it was the injustice and oppression of these great men which has commonly brought them into contempt with the people. The craft and art of such men are great, and who that is the least acquainted with history or with law can be ignorant of the specious pretenses which have often been made use of by men in power to introduce arbitrary rule and destroy the liberties of a free people? . . .

What Is Libel?

And may not I be allowed . . . to say that, by a little countenance, almost anything which a man writes may, with the help of that useful term of art called an innuendo, be construed to be a libel, according to Mr. Attorney's definition of it; that whether the words are spoken of a person of a public character, or of a private man, whether dead or living, good or bad, true or false, all make a libel; for, according to Mr. Attorney, after a man hears a writing read, or reads and repeats it, or laughs at it, they are all punishable. It is true, Mr. Attorney is so good as to allow, after the party knows it to be a libel; but he is not so kind as to take the man's word for it.

If a libel is understood in the large and unlimited sense urged by Mr. Attorney, there is scarce a writing I know that may not be called a libel, or scarce any person safe from being called to account as a libeler; for Moses, meek as he was, libeled Cain; and who is it that has not libeled the devil? For, according to Mr. Attorney, it is no justification to say one has a bad name. . . . How must a man speak or write, or what must he hear, read, or sing? Or when must he laugh, so as to

Printers throughout the colonies resumed their work without fear following Hamilton's landmark victory securing freedom of speech and of the press.

be secure from being taken up as a libeler? I sincerely believe that were some persons to go through the streets of New York nowadays and read a part of the Bible, if it were not known to be such, Mr. Attorney, with the help of his innuendos, would easily turn it into a libel. As for instance: Isaiah xi. 16. "The leaders of the people cause them to err, and they that are led by them are destroyed." But should Mr. Attorney go about to make this a libel, he would read it thus: "The leaders of the people" (*innuendo*, the Governor and council of New York) "cause them" (*innuendo*, the people of this province) "to err, and they" (the Governor and council meaning) "are destroyed"(*innuendo*, are deceived into the loss of their liberty), "which is the worst kind of destruction." Or if some person should publicly repeat, in a manner not pleasing to his betters, the tenth and the eleventh verses of the fifty-sixth chapter of the same book, there Mr. Attorney would have a large field to display his skill in the artful application of his innuendos. The words are: "His watchmen are blind, they are ignorant," etc. "Yea, they are greedy dogs, they can never have enough." But to make them a libel, there is, according to Mr. Attorney's doctrine, no more wanting but the aid of his skill in the right adapting his innuendos. As, for instance, "His watchmen" (*innuendo*, the Governor's council and assembly) "are blind, they are ignorant" (*innuendo*, will not see the dangerous designs of his Excellency). "Yea, they" (the Governor and council, meaning) "are greedy dogs, which can never have enough" (*innuendo*, enough of riches and power). Such an instance as this seems only fit to be laughed at, but I may appeal to Mr. Attorney himself whether these are not at least equally proper to be applied to his Excellency and his ministers as some of the inferences and innuendos in his information against my client. Then, if Mr. Attorney be at liberty to come into court and file an information in the King's name without leave, who is secure whom he is pleased to prosecute as a libeler? And as the crown law is contended for in bad times, there is no remedy for the greatest oppression of this sort, even though the party prosecuted be acquitted with honor. And give me leave to say, as great men as any in Britain have boldly asserted that the mode of prosecuting by information (when a grand jury will not find *billa vera*[1]) is a national grievance and greatly inconsistent with that freedom which the subjects of England enjoy in most other cases. But if we are so unhappy as not to be able to ward off this stroke of power directly, let us take care not to be cheated out of our liberties by forms and appearances; let us always be sure that the charge in the information is made out clearly, even beyond a doubt; for, though matters in the information may be called form upon trial, yet they may be, and often have been found to be, matters of substance upon giving judgment.

The Value of Liberty

Gentlemen, the danger is great in proportion to the mischief that may happen through our too great credulity. A proper confidence in a court is commendable, but as the verdict (whatever it is) will be yours, you ought to refer no part of your duty to the discretion of other persons. If you should be of opinion that there is no falsehood in Mr. Zenger's papers, you will, nay, (pardon me for the expression) you ought to say so; because you do not know whether others (I mean the court) may be of that opinion. It is your right to do so, and there is much depending upon your resolution, as well as upon your integrity.

The loss of liberty to a generous mind is worse than death; and yet we know there have been those in all ages who, for the sake of preferment, or some imaginary honor, have freely lent a helping hand to oppress, nay, to destroy their country. This brings to my mind that saying of the immortal Brutus, when he looked upon the creatures of Caesar, who were very great men, but by no means good men: "You Romans," said Brutus, "if yet I may call you so, consider what you are doing; remember that you are assisting Caesar to forge those very chains which one day he will make yourselves wear." This is what every man that values freedom ought to consider; he should act by judgment and not by affection or self-interest; for where those prevail, no ties of ei-

---

1. "Billa vera," or "true bill," is written on a bill of indictment during a grand jury trial when the jury, having heard the state witnesses, believe that sufficient cause has been shown to proceed with the trial of the defendant.

ther country or kindred are regarded; as upon the other hand, the man who loves his country prefers its liberty to all other considerations, well knowing that without liberty life is a misery. . . .

Power Must Be Controlled

Power may justly be compared to a great river; while kept within its bounds, it is both beautiful and useful, but when it overflows its banks, it is then too impetuous to be stemmed; it bears down all before it, and brings destruction and desolation wherever it comes. If, then, this be the nature of power, let us at least do our duty, and, like wise men who value freedom, use our utmost care to support liberty, the only bulwark against lawless power, which, in all ages, has sacrificed to its wild lust and boundless ambition the blood of the best men that ever lived.

I hope to be pardoned, sir, for my zeal upon this occasion. It is an old and wise caution that "when our neighbor's house is on fire, we ought to take care of our own." For though, blessed be God, I live in a government where liberty is well understood and freely enjoyed, yet experience has shown us all (I am sure it has to me) that a bad precedent in one government is soon set up for an authority in another; and therefore I cannot but think it mine, and every honest man's duty, that, while we pay all due obedience to men in authority, we ought, at the same time, to be upon our guard against power wherever we apprehend that it may affect ourselves or our fellow-subjects.

I am truly very unequal to such an undertaking, on many accounts. And you see I labor under the weight of many years and am borne down with great infirmities of body; yet old and weak as I am, I should think it my duty, if required, to go to the utmost part of the land, where my service could be of any use in assisting to quench the flame of prosecutions upon informations, set on foot by the Government to deprive a people of the right of remonstrating, and complaining too, of the arbitrary attempts of men in power. Men who injure and oppress the people under their administration provoke them to cry out and complain, and then make that very complaint the foundation for new oppressions and prosecutions. I wish I could say there were no instances of this kind. But, to conclude, the question before the court, and you, gentlemen of the jury, is not of small nor private concern; it is not the cause of a poor printer, nor of New York alone, which you are now trying. No! It may, in its consequence, affect every free man that lives under a British Government on the main continent of America. It is the best cause; it is the cause of liberty; and I make no doubt but your upright conduct, this day, will not only entitle you to the love and esteem of your fellow-citizen, but every man who prefers freedom to a life of slavery will bless and honor you as men who have baffled the attempt of tyranny, and, by an impartial and uncorrupt verdict, have laid a noble foundation for securing to ourselves, our posterity, and our neighbors, that to which nature and the laws of our country have given us a right—the liberty both of exposing and opposing arbitrary power (in these parts of the world, at least) by speaking and writing truth.

Liberty Lies in Obedience to the Law

Jonathon Boucher

In 1762, Jonathon Boucher was ordained by the Church
of England and began his duties as a rector in Virginia.
Boucher was an Englishman (he had lived in Virginia for
only three years previously) who was ardently loyal to
the British Crown and was thus appalled by the rebellious activities in the colonies. An eloquent and educated
person with a captive audience of parishioners, Boucher
made it his duty to espouse the Loyalist cause in his
weekly sermons. In the 1760s and 1770s, however, these
views were not popular, and the following speech given in
1775 was one of Boucher's last before he was finally
forced to return to England. Upon his return to Europe,
he published these sermons under the title of *A View of
the Causes and Consequence of the Revolution.*

In the following excerpts from his sermon entitled
"On Civil Liberty, Passive Obedience, and Nonresis-
tance," Boucher contends that liberty consists in sub-
servience to the law, for freedom has no meaning outside
the structures of government. "Obedience to government
is every man's duty," Boucher argues. Moreover, because
governments are divinely empowered, to resist authority
is akin to resisting God. Boucher urges those who believe
their government has become oppressive not to resist or
rebel. Instead, they should petition the government and
accept whatever outcome results. Such pessimism and
passivity ran deeply counter to the empowered, activist

From Jonathon Boucher, "On Civil Liberty, Passive Obedience, and Nonresis-
tance," delivered in Maryland, 1775, as reprinted in *American Voices: Significant
Speeches in American History, 1640–1945,* edited by James Andrews and David
Zarefsky (New York: Longman, 1989).

approach that characterized most of the American colonists, and men such as Boucher provided ready examples of all that the patriots rejected.

Obedience to government is every man's duty, because it is every man's interest; but it is particularly incumbent on Christians, because (in addition to its moral fitness) it is enjoined by the positive commands of God; and, therefore, when Christians are disobedient to human ordinances, they are also disobedient to God. If the form of government under which the good providence of God has been pleased to place us be mild and free, it is our duty to enjoy it with gratitude and with thankfulness and, in particular, to be careful not to abuse it by licentiousness. If it be less indulgent and less liberal than in reason it ought to be, still it is our duty not to disturb and destroy the peace of the community by becoming refractory and rebellious subjects and *resisting the ordinances of God*. However humiliating such acquiescence may seem to men of warm and eager minds, the wisdom of God in having made it our duty is manifest. For, as it is the natural temper and bias of the human mind to be impatient under restraint, it was wise and merciful in the blessed Author of our religion not to add any new impulse to the natural force of this prevailing propensity but, with the whole weight of his authority, altogether to discountenance every tendency to disobedience. . . .

The Law Ensures Liberty

To respect the laws is to respect liberty in the only rational sense in which the term can be used, for liberty consists in a subserviency to law. "Where there is no law," says Mr. [John] Locke, "there is no freedom." The mere man of nature (if such an one there ever was) has no freedom: *all his lifetime he is subject to bondage*. It is by being included within the pale of civil polity and government that he takes his rank in society as a free man.

Hence it follows that we are free, or otherwise, as we are

governed by law, or by the mere arbitrary will, or wills, of any individual, or any number of individuals. And liberty is not the setting at nought and despising established laws— much less the making our own wills the rule of our own actions, or the actions of others—and not bearing (whilst yet we dictate to others) the being dictated to, even by the laws of the land; but it is the being governed by law and by law only. . . . The more carefully well-devised restraints of law are enacted, and the more rigorously they are executed in any country, the greater degree of civil liberty does that country enjoy. To pursue liberty, then, in a manner not warranted by law, whatever the pretense may be, is clearly to be hostile to liberty; and those persons who thus *promise you liberty* are themselves *the servants of corruption.*

"Civil liberty (says an excellent writer) is a severe and a restrained thing; implies, in the notion of it, authority, settled subordinations, subjection, and obedience; and is altogether as much hurt by too little of this kind, as by too much of it. And the love of liberty, when it is indeed the love of liberty, which carries us to withstand tyranny, will as much carry us to reverence authority, and to support it; for this most obvious reason, that one is as necessary to the being of liberty, as the other is destructive of it. And, therefore, the love of liberty which does not produce this effect, the love of liberty which is not a real principle of dutiful behavior toward authority, is as hypocritical as the religion which is not productive of a good life. Licentiousness is, in truth, such an excess of liberty as is of the same nature with tyranny. For, what is the difference betwixt them, but that one is lawless power exercised under pretense of authority, or by persons vested with it; the other, lawless power exercised under pretense of liberty, or without any pretense at all? A people, then, must always be less free in proportion as they are more licentious, licentiousness being not only different from liberty but directly contrary to it—a direct breach upon it."

True liberty, then, is a liberty to do everything that is right, and the being restrained from doing anything that is wrong. So far from our having a right to do everything that we please, under a notion of liberty, liberty itself is limited and confined—but limited and confined only by laws which are at the same time both its foundation and its support. It can, however, hardly be necessary to inform you that ideas and notions respecting liberty, very different from these, are daily suggested in the speeches and the writings of the times; and also that some opinions on the subject of government at large, which apear to me to be particularly loose and dangerous, are advanced in the sermon now under consideration; and that, therefore, you will acknowledge the propriety of my bestowing some farther notice on them both.

It is laid down in this sermon, as a settled maxim, that the end of government is "the common good of mankind." I am not sure that the position itself is indisputable; but, if it were, it would by no means follow that "this common good being matter of common feeling, government must therefore have been instituted by common consent." There is an appearance of logical accuracy and precision in this statement; but it is only an appearance. The position is vague and loose; and the assertion is made without an attempt to prove it. If by men's "common feelings" we are to understand that principle in the human mind called common sense, the assertion is either unmeaning and insignificant, or it is false. In no instance have mankind ever yet agreed as to what is, or is not, "the common good." A form or mode of government cannot be named, which these "common feelings" and "common consent," the sole arbiters, as it seems, of "common good," have not, at one time or another, set up and established, and again pulled down and reprobated. What one people in one age have concurred in establishing as the "common good," another in another age have voted to be mischievous and big with ruin. The premises, therefore, that "the common good is matter of common feeling," being false, the consequence drawn from it, viz., that government was instituted by "common consent," is of course equally false.

Men Are Not Equal

This popular notion, that government was originally formed by the consent or by a compact of the people, rests on, and is supported by, another similar notion, not less popular, nor better founded. This other notion is that the whole human race is born equal; and that no man is naturally inferior, or, in any respect, subjected to another; and that he can be made subject to another only by his own consent. The position is equally ill-founded and false both in its premises and conclusions. In hardly any sense that can be imagined is the position strictly true; but, as applied to the case under consideration, it is demonstrably not true. Man differs from man in everything that can be supposed to lead to supremacy and subjection, *as one star differs from another star in glory*. It was the purpose of the Creator that man should be social; but, without government, there can be no society; nor, without some relative inferiority and superiority, can there be any government. A musical instrument composed of chords, keys, or pipes, all perfectly equal in size and power, might as well be expected to produce harmony, as a society composed of members all perfectly equal to be productive of order and peace. If (according to the idea of the advocates of this chimerical scheme of equality) no man could rightfully *be compelled to come in* and be a member even of a government to be formed by a regular compact, but by his own individual consent, it clearly follows, from the same principles, that neither could he rightfully be made or compelled to submit to the ordinances of any government already formed, to which he has not individually or actually consented. On the principle of equality, neither his parents, nor even the vote of a majority of the society (however virtuously and honorably that vote might be obtained), can have any such authority over any man. Neither can it be mantained that acquiescence implies consent; because acquiescence may have been extorted from impotence or incapacity. Even an explicit consent can bind a man no longer than he chooses to be bound. The same principle of equality that exempts him from being governed without his own consent clearly entitles him to recall and resume that consent whenever he sees fit; and he alone has a right to judge when and for what reasons it may be resumed.

The Social Compact

Any attempt, therefore, to introduce this fantastic system into practice would reduce the whole business of social life to the wearisome, confused, and useless task of mankind's first expressing, and then withdrawing, their consent to an endless succession of schemes of government. Governments, though always forming, would never be completely formed; for the majority today might be the minority tomorrow, and, of course, that which is now fixed might and would be soon unfixed. Mr. Locke indeed says that, "by consenting with others to make one body-politic under government, a man puts himself under an obligation to every one of that society to submit to the determination of the majority, and to be concluded by it." For the sake of the peace of society, it is undoubtedly reasonable and necessary that this should be the case; but, on the principles of the system now under consideration, before Mr. Locke or any of his followers can have authority to say that it actually is the case, it must be stated and proved that every individual man, on entering into the social compact, did first consent, and declare his consent, to be concluded and bound in all cases by the vote of the majority. In making such a declaration, he would certainly consult both his interest and his duty; but at the same time he would also completely relinquish the principle of equality, and eventually subject himself to the possibility of being governed by ignorant and corrupt tyrants. Mr. Locke himself afterward disproves his own position respecting this supposed obligation to submit to the "determination of the majority," when he argues that a right of resistance still exists in the governed; for, what is resistance but a recalling and resuming the consent heretofore supposed to have been given, and in fact refusing to submit to the "determination of the majority"? It does not clearly appear what Mr. Locke exactly meant by what he calls "the determination of the majority"; but the only rational and practical public manner of declaring "the determination of the majority" is by law: the laws, therefore, in all countries, even in those that are despotically governed, are to be regarded as the declared "determination of a majority" of the members of that community; because, in such cases, even acquiescence only must be looked upon as equivalent to a declaration. A right of resistance, therefore, for which Mr. Locke contends, is incompatible with the duty of submitting to the determination of "the majority," for which he also contends. . . .

Kings Are God's Agents

The glory of God is much concerned that there should be good government in the world; it is, therefore, the uniform doctrine of the Scriptures that it is under the deputation and authority of God alone that *kings reign and princes decree justice.* Kings and princes (which are only other words for supreme magistrates) were doubtless created and appointed, not so much for their own sakes, as for the sake of the people committed to their charge; yet are they not, therefore, the creatures of the people. So far from deriving their authority from any supposed consent or suffrage of men, they receive their commission from Heaven; they receive it from God, the source and original of all power. However obsolete, therefore, either the sentiment or the language may now be deemed, it is with the most perfect propriety that the supreme magistrate, whether consisting of one or of many, and whether denominated an emperor, a king, an archon, a dictator, a consul, or a senate, is to be regarded and venerated as the vicegerent of God.

Patience in Times of Bad Government

Nor let this be deemed a degrading and servile principle: it is the very reverse; and it is this its superior dignity which proves its celestial origin. For, whilst other doctrines and other systems distract the world with disputes and debates which admit of no decision, and of *wars and fightings* which are almost as endless as they are useless, it is the glory of Christianity to teach her votaries patiently to bear imperfections, inconveniences, and evils in government, as in everything else that is human. This patient acquiescence under some remediless evils is not more our duty than it is our interest: for, the only very intolerable grievance in government is when men allow themselves to disturb and destroy the peace of the world by vain attempts to render that perfect which the laws of our nature have ordained to the imperfect. And there is more magnanimity, as well as more wisdom, in enduring some present and certain evils than can be manifested by any projects of redress that are uncertain; but which, if they fail, may bring down irretrievable ruin on thousands of others, as well as on ourselves, since to suffer nobly indicates more greatness of mind than can be shown even by acting valiantly. Wise men, therefore, in the words of a noted philosopher, will "rather choose to brook with patience some inconveniences under government" (because human affairs cannot possibly be without some) than self-opinionatedly disturb the quiet of the public. And, weighing the justice of those things you are about, not by the persuasion and advice of private men, but by the laws of the realm, you will no longer suffer ambitious men, through the streams of your blood, to wade to their own power but esteem it better to enjoy ourselves in the present state, though perhaps not the best, than, by waging war, endeavor to procure a reformation. . . .

Passive Obedience

All government, whether lodged in one or in many, is, in its nature, absolute and irresistible. It is not within the competency even of the supreme power to limit itself, because such limitation can emanate only from a superior. For any government to make itself irresistible, and to cease to be absolute, it must cease to be supreme, which is but saying, in other words, that it must dissolve itself or be destroyed. If, then, to resist government be to destroy it, every man who is a subject must necessarily owe to the government under which he lives an obedience either active or passive: active, where the duty enjoined may be performed without offending God; and passive (that is to say, patiently to submit to the penalties annexed to disobedience), where that which is commanded by man is forbidden by God. No government upon earth can rightfully compel any one of its subjects to an active compliance with anything that is, or that appears to his conscience to be, inconsistent with, or contradictory to, the known laws of God, because every man is under a prior and superior obligation to *obey God in all things*. When such cases of incompatible demands of duty occur, every well-informed person knows what he is to do; and every well-principled person will do what he ought, viz., he will submit to the ordinances of God rather than comply with the commandments of men. In thus acting, he cannot err, and this alone is "passive obedience," which I entreat you to observe is so far from being "unlimited obedience" (as its enemies wilfully persist to miscall it) that it is the direct contrary. Resolute not to disobey God, a man of good principles determines, in case of competition, as the lesser evil, to disobey man; but he knows that he should also disobey God, were he not, at the same time, patiently to submit to any penalties incurred by his disobedience to man. . . .

Resistance Leads to Rebellion

Be it (for the sake of argument) admitted that the government under which till now you have lived happily is, most unaccountably, all at once become *oppressive and severe;* did you, of yourselves, make the discovery? No. I affirm, without any apprehension of being contradicted, that you are acquainted with these oppressions only from the report of others. For what, then (admitting you have a right to resist in any case), are you now urged to resist and rise against those whom you have hitherto always regarded (and certainly not without reason) as your *nursing fathers and nursing mothers?* Often as you have already heard it repeated without expressing any disapprobation, I assure myself it will afford you no pleasure to be reminded that it is on account of an insignificant duty on tea, imposed by the British Parliament, and which, for aught we know, may or may not be constitutionally imposed, but which, we well know, two-thirds of the people of America can never be called on to pay. Is it the part of an *understanding people,* of loyal subjects, or of good Christians, instantly to resist and rebel for a cause so trivial? O my brethren, consult your own hearts and follow your own judgments! and learn not your "measures of obedience" from men who weakly or wickedly imagine there can be liberty unconnected with law—and whose aim it is to drive you on, step by step, to a resistance which will terminate, if it does not begin, in rebellion! On all such trying occasions, learn the line of conduct which it is your duty and interest to observe, from our constitution itself, which, in this particular, is a fair transcript or exemplification of the ordinance of God. Both the one and the other warn you against resistance; but you are not forbidden either to remonstrate or to petition. And can it be humiliating to any man, or any number of men, to ask when we have but to *ask and it shall be given?* Is prayer an abject duty, or do men ever appear either so great, or so amiable, as when they are modest and humble? However meanly this privilege of petitioning may be regarded by those who claim everything as a right, they are challenged to show an instance in which it has failed when it ought to have succeeded. If, however, our grievances, in any point of view, be of such moment as that other means of obtaining redress should be judged expedient, happily we enjoy those means. In a certain sense, some considerable portion of legislation is still in our own hands. We are supposed to have chosen "fit and able" persons to represent us in the great council of our country; and they only can constitutionally interfere either to obtain the enacting of what is right or the repeal of what is wrong. If we, and our fellow-subjects, have been conscientiously faithful in the discharge of our duty, we can have no reason to doubt that our delegates will be equally faithful in the discharge of theirs. Our provincial assemblies, it is true, are but one part of our colonial legislature; they form, however, that part which is the most efficient. If the present general topic of complaint be in their estimation, well founded, and a real and great grievance, what reason have you to imagine that all the assemblies on the continent will not concur and be unanimous in so representing it? And if they should all concur so to represent it, it is hardly within the reach of supposition that all due attention will not be paid to their united remonstrances. So many and such large concessions have often been made, at the instance only of individual assemblies, that we are warranted in relying that nothing which is reasonable and proper will ever be withheld from us, provided only it be asked for with decency, and that we do not previously forfeit our title to attention by becoming refractory and rebellious.

Let it be supposed, however, that even the worst may happen, which can happen: that our remonstrances are disregarded, our petitions rejected, and our grievances unredressed: what, you will naturally ask—what, in such a case, would I advise you to do? . . . To your question, therefore, I hesitate not to answer that I wish and advise you to act the part of reasonable men and of Christians. You will be pleased to observe, however, that I am far from thinking that your virtue will ever be brought to so severe a test and trial. The question, I am aware, was an ensnaring one, suggested to you by those who are as little solicitous about your peace as they are for my safety; the answer which, in condescension to your wishes, I have given to it is direct and plain and not more applicable to you than it is to all the people of America. If you think the duty of three pence a pound upon tea laid on by the British Parliament a grievance, it is your duty to instruct your members to take all the constitutional means in their power to obtain redress; if those means fail of success, you cannot but be sorry and grieved, but you will better bear your disappointment by being able to reflect that it was not owing to any misconduct of your own. And, what is the whole history of human life, public or private, but a series of disappointments? It might be hoped that Christians would not think it grievous to be doomed to submit to disappointments and calamities, as their Master submitted, even if they were as innocent. His disciples and first followers shrunk from no trials nor dangers. Treading in the steps of him who, *when he was reviled, blessed, and when he was persecuted, suffered it,* they willingly laid down their lives rather than resist some of the worst tyrants that ever disgraced the annals of history. Those persons are as little acquainted with general history, as they are with the particular doctrines of Christianity, who represent such submission as abject and servile. I affirm, with great authority, that "there can be no better way of asserting the people's lawful rights, than the disowning unlawful commands, by thus patiently suffering." When this doctrine was more generally embraced, our holy religion gained as much by submission as it is now in a fair way of losing for want of it.

Liberty Lies in Independence from Great Britain

Samuel Adams

In this seminal speech, one of the most important figures of the Revolutionary era offers a vehement and passionate set of arguments for why American independence from Great Britain is both necessary and desirable. Known as the "Father of the American Revolution" for his tireless efforts to promote American Independence, Samuel Adams was elected to the state legislature in 1766. In this position, he worked to combat British policies not only at a governmental level but also as an effective grassroots organizer and propagandist among the people of Boston.

When Adams delivered this speech in August of 1776, the British forces had already been victorious against the Americans in the Battle of Bunker Hill on June 17, 1775. Back in Philadelphia, at the Second Continental Congress, delegates were split between those like Patrick Henry (the "Liberty or Death" orator) who were calling for military preparations and moderates such as John Dickinson (a gentleman farmer and politician from Pennsylvania) who were still hoping to avert war. In a last desperate attempt, Dickinson authored his "Olive Branch Petition" as a final plea for reconciliation.

However, by the time King George received the petition for peace, he had already been informed of the Bunker Hill fighting in which the British, despite their victory, had lost over one thousand soldiers. He angrily

From Samuel Adams, "American Independence," delivered at the State House in Philadelphia, Pennsylvania, August 1, 1776, as reprinted in *Early American Orations, 1760–1824*, edited by Louie R. Heller (New York: Macmillan, 1902).

declared the colonies to be in a state of rebellion. At this
point, armed conflict was inevitable, and by mid-1776,
the congressional delegates were working on the Declaration of Independence. Thomas Jefferson was assigned the
responsibility of drawing up a draft, Congress approved
the Declaration in its vote of July 2, and after several
amendments (including the deletion of Jefferson's clauses
condemning slavery), the Declaration was approved on
July 4, 1776. Samuel Adams delivered the following
speech less than a month after the historic Declaration,
and his tone matches the enthusiasm and inspiring patriotism of the day.

Our forefathers threw off the yoke of Popery in religion; for you is reserved the levelling the popery of
politics. They opened the Bible to all, and maintained
the capacity of every man to judge for himself in religion. Are
we sufficient for the comprehension of the sublimest spiritual
truths, and unequal to material and temporal ones? Heaven
hath trusted us with the management of things for eternity,
and man denies us ability to judge of the present, or to know
from our feelings the experience that will make us happy.
"You can discern," say they, "objects distant and remote, but
cannot perceive those within your grasp. Let us leave the distribution of present goods, and cut out and manage as you
please the interests of futurity." This day, I trust, the reign of
political protestantism will commence. We have explored the
temple of royalty, and found that the idol we have bowed
down to has eyes which see not, ears that hear not our
prayers, and a heart like the nether millstone. We have this
day restored the Sovereign, to whom alone men ought to be
obedient. He reigns in Heaven, and with a propitious eye beholds his subjects assuming that freedom of thought and dignity of self-direction which He bestowed on them. From the
rising to the setting sun may His kingdom come.
    Having been a slave to the influence of opinions early
acquired and distinctions generally received, I am ever inclined not to despise but to pity those who are yet in dark-

ness. But to the eye of reason what can be more clear than that all men have an equal right to happiness? Nature made no other distinction than that of higher or lower degrees of power of mind and body. But what mysterious distribution of character has the craft of statesmen, more fatal than priestcraft, introduced?

According to their doctrine, the offspring of a successful invader shall, from generation to generation, arrogate the right of lavishing on their pleasures a proportion of the fruits of the earth, more than sufficient to supply the wants of thousands of their fellow-creatures; claim authority to manage them like beasts of burthen; and without superior industry, capacity, or virtue,—nay, though disgraceful to humanity by their ignorance, intemperance, and brutality,—shall be deemed best calculated to frame laws and to consult for the welfare of society.

Were the talents and virtues which Heaven has bestowed upon men given merely to make them more obedient drudges, to be sacrificed to the follies and ambitions of the few? or were not the noble gifts so equally dispensed with a divine purpose and law that they should as nearly as possible be equally exerted, and the blessings of poverty be equally enjoyed by all? Away, then, with those absurd systems which, to gratify the pride of a few, debase the greatest part of our species below the order of men. What an affront to the King of the universe, to maintain that the happiness of a monster sunk in debauchery and spreading desolation and murder among men, of a Caligula, a Nero, or a Charles, is more precious in His sight than that of millions of His suppliant creatures, who do justice, love mercy, and walk humbly with their God! No! in the judgment of Heaven there is no other superiority among men than a superiority in wisdom and virtue. And can we have a safer model in forming ours? The Deity, then, has not given any order or family of men authority over others, and if any men have given it, they only could give it for themselves. Our forefathers, 'tis said, consented to be subject to the laws of Great Britain. I will not, at present, dispute it, nor mark out the limits and conditions of their submission; but will it be denied that they contracted to pay obedience, and to be under the control of Great

Britain, because it appeared to them most beneficial in their then present circumstances and situations? We, my country-men, have the same right to consult and provide for our hap-piness which they had to promote theirs. If they had a view to posterity in their contracts, it must have been to advance the felicity of their descendants. If they erred in their expec-tations and prospects, we can never be condemned for a con-duct which they would have recommended had but they fore-seen our present condition.

Ye darkeners of counsel, who would make the property, lives, and religion of millions depend on the evasive interpre-tations of musty parchments; who would send us to anti-quated charters, of uncertain and contradictory meaning, to prove that the present generation are not bound to be victims to cruel and unforgiving despotism, tell us whether our pious and generous ancestors bequeathed to us the miserable priv-ilege of having the rewards of our honest industry, the fruits of those fields which they purchased and bled for, wrested from us at the will of men over whom we have no check? Did they contract for us that, with folded arms, we should expect that justice and mercy from brutal and inflamed invaders which have been denied to our supplications at the foot of the throne? Were we to hear our character as a people ridiculed with indifference? Did they promise for us that our meekness and patience should be insulted; our coasts ha-rassed; our towns demolished and plundered, and our wives and offspring exposed to nakedness, hunger, and death, with-out our feeling the resentment of men, and exerting those powers of self-preservation which God has given us? No man had once a greater veneration for Englishmen than I enter-tained. They were dear to me, as branches of the same parental trunk, and partakers of the same religion and laws; I still view with respect the remains of the constitution as I would a lifeless body which had once been animated by a great and heroic soul. But when I am roused by the din of arms; when I behold legions of foreign assassins, paid by Englishmen to imbrue their hands in our blood; when I tread over the uncoffined bones of my countrymen, neighbors, and friends; when I see the locks of a venerable father torn by savage hands, and a feeble mother, clasping her infants to her bosom, on her knees imploring their lives from her own slaves, whom Englishmen have allured to treachery and murder; when I behold my country, once the seat of industry, peace, and plenty changed by Englishmen to a theatre of blood and misery, Heaven forgive me if I cannot root out those passions which it has implanted in my bosom, and detest submission to a people who have either ceased to be human, or have not virtue enough to feel their own wretchedness and servitude. . . .

We Are No Longer Dependent on Britain

The doctrine of dependence upon Great Britain is, I believe, generally exploded; but as I would attend to the honest weakness of the simplest of men, you will pardon me if I offer a few words on this subject.

We are now on this continent, to the astonishment of the world, three millions of souls united in one common cause. We have large armies well disciplined and appointed, with commanders inferior to none in military skill, and superior in activity and zeal. We are furnished with arsenals and stores beyond our most sanguine expectations, and foreign nations are waiting to crown our success with their alliances. There are instances of, I would say, an almost astonishing Providence in our favor; our success has staggered our enemies, and almost given faith to infidels; so that we may truly say it is not our own arm which has saved us.

The hand of Heaven seems to have led us on to be, perhaps, humble instruments and means in the great Providential dispensation which is completing. We have fled from the political Sodom; let us not look back lest we perish and become a monument of infamy and derision to the world. For can we ever expect more unanimity and a better preparation for defense; more infatuation of counsel among our enemies, and more valor and zeal among ourselves? The same force and resistance which are sufficient to procure us our liberties, will secure us a glorious independence and support us in the dignity of free, imperial States. We cannot suppose that our opposition has made a corrupt and dissipated nation more friendly to America, or created in them

a greater respect for the rights of mankind. We can, therefore, expect a restoration and establishment of our privileges, and a compensation for the injuries we have received
from their want of power, from their fears, and not from
their virtues. The unanimity and valor which will affect all
honorable peace can render a future contest for our liberties unnecessary. He who has strength to chain down the
wolf, is a madman if he lets him loose without drawing his
teeth and paring his nails.

From the day on which an accommodation takes place
between England and America on any other terms than as independent states, I shall date the ruin of this country. A
politic minister will study to lull us into security by granting
us the full extent of our petitions. The warm sunshine of influence would melt down the virtue which the violence of the
storm rendered more firm and unyielding. In a state of tranquillity, wealth, and luxury, our descendants would forget
the arts of war and the noble activity and zeal which made
their ancestors invincible. Every art of corruption would be
employed to loosen the bond of union which renders our resistance formidable. When the spirit of liberty which now an-
imates our hearts and gives success to our arms is extinct, our
numbers will accelerate our ruin, and render us easier victims
to tyranny. Ye abandoned minions of all infatuated ministry,
if peradventure any should yet remain among us—remember
that a Warren and a Montgomery [American patriots already
killed in the fighting] are numbered among the dead! Contemplate the mangled bodies of your countrymen and then
say, what should be the reward of such sacrifices? Bid not our
posterity bow the knee, supplicate the friendship, and plough
and sow and reap, to glut the avarice of the men who have
let loose on us the dogs of war to riot in our blood, and hunt
us from the face of the earth! If ye love wealth better than liberty, the tranquillity of servitude than the animating contest
of freedom, go from us in peace. We ask not your counsels or
arms. Crouch down and lick the hands which feed you. May
your chains set lightly upon you, and may posterity forget
that ye were our countrymen.

To unite the *Supremacy of Great Britain* and the *Liberty
of America* is utterly impossible. So vast a continent and at

such a distance from the seat of empire, will every day grow more unmanageable. The motion of so unwieldy a body cannot be directed with any dispatch and uniformity, without committing to the Parliament of Great Britain powers inconsistent with our freedom. The authority and force which would be absolutely necessary for the preservation of the peace and good order of this continent would put all our valuable rights within the reach of that nation.

As the administration of government requires firmer and more numerous supports in proportion to its extent, the burthens imposed on us would be excessive, and we should leave the melancholy prospect of their increasing on our posterity. The scale of officers, from the rapacious and needy commissioner, to the haughty governor, and from the governor with his hungry train to perhaps a licentious and prodigal viceroy, must be upheld by you and your children. The fleets and armies which will be employed to silence your murmurs and complaints must be supported by the fruits of your industry.

And yet, with all this enlargement of the expense and powers of government, the administration of it at such a distance and over so extensive a territory, must necessarily fail of putting the laws into vigorous execution, removing private oppressions, and forming plans for the advancement of agriculture and commerce, and preserving the vast empire in any tolerable peace and security. If our posterity retain any spark of patriotism, they can never tamely submit to any such burthens. This country will be made the field of bloody contention till it gains that independence for which nature formed it. It is, therefore, injustice and cruelty to our offspring, and would stamp us with the character of baseness and cowardice, to leave the salvation of this country to be worked out by them with accumulated difficulty and danger. . . .

We Must Break Free

Other nations have received their laws from conquerors; some are indebted for a constitution to the sufferings of their ancestors through revolving centuries. The people of this country alone have formally and deliberately chosen a government for themselves, and with open and uninfluenced consent bound themselves to a social compact. Here no man proclaims his birth or wealth as a title to honorable distinction or to sanctify ignorance and vice with the name of hereditary authority. He who has most zeal and ability to promote public felicity, let him be the servant of the public. This is the only line of distinction drawn by nature. Leave the bird of night to the obscurity for which nature intended him, and expect only from the eagle to burst the clouds with his wings and look boldly in the face of the sun.

Some who would persuade us that they have tender feelings for future generations, while they are insensible to the happiness of the present, are perpetually foreboding a train of dissensions under our popular system. Such men's reasoning amounts to this: give up all that is valuable to Great Britain, and then you will have no inducements to quarrel among yourselves; or suffer yourselves to be chained down by your enemies, that you may not be able to fight with your friends.

This is an insult on your virtue as well as your common sense. Your unanimity this day and through the course of the war is a decisive refutation of such invidious predictions. Our enemies have already had evidence that our present constitution contains in it the justice and ardor of freedom, and the wisdom and vigor of the most absolute system. When the law is the will of the people, it will be uniform and coherent; but fluctuation, contradiction, and inconsistency of councils must be expected under those governments where every revolution in the ministry of a court produces one in the state. Such being the folly and pride of all ministers, that they ever pursue measures directly opposite to those of their predecessors.

We shall neither be exposed to the necessary convulsions of elective monarchies, nor to the want of wisdom, fortitude, and virtue to which hereditary succession is liable. In your hands it will be to perpetuate a prudent, active, and just legislature, which will never expire until you yourselves lose the virtues which give it existence. . . .

Independence or Servitude!

We have now no other alternative than independence, or the most ignominious and galling servitude. The legions of our enemies thicken on our plains; desolation and death mark their bloody career; whilst the mangled corpses of our countrymen seem to cry out to us as a voice from heaven: "Will you permit our posterity to groan under the galling chains of our murderers? Has our blood been expended in vain? Is the only reward which our constancy till death has obtained for our country, that it should be sunk into a deeper and more ignominious vassalage? Recollect who are the men that demand your submission; to whose decrees you are invited to pay obedience. Men who, unmindful of their relation to you as brethren, of your long implicit submission to their laws, of the sacrifice which you and your forefathers made of your natural advantages for commerce to their avarice—formed a deliberate plan to wrest from you the small pittance of property which they had permitted you to acquire. Remember that the men who wish to rule over you are they who, in pursuit of this plan of despotism, annulled the sacred contracts which had been made with your ancestors; conveyed into your cities a mercenary soldiery to compel you to submission by insult and murder—who called your patience, cowardice; your piety, hypocrisy."

Countrymen, the men who now invite you to surrender your rights into their hands, are the men who have let loose the merciless savages to riot in the blood of their brethren; who have dared to establish popery triumphant in our land; who have taught treachery to your slaves, and courted them to assassinate your wives and children.

These are the men to whom we are exhorted to sacrifice the blessings which Providence holds out to us,—the happiness, the dignity of uncontrolled freedom and independence.

Let not your generous indignation be directed against any among us, who may advise so absurd and maddening a measure. Their number is but few and daily decreases; and the spirit which can render them patient of slavery, will render them contemptible enemies.

Our Union is now complete; our Constitution composed, established, and approved. You are now the guardians of your own liberties. We may justly address you as the Decemviri did the Romans, and say: "Nothing that we propose can pass into a law without your consent. Be yourselves, O Americans, the authors of those laws on which your happiness depends."

You have now in the field armies sufficient to repel the whole force of your enemies and their base and mercenary auxiliaries. The hearts of your soldiers beat high with the spirit of freedom; they are animated with the justice of their cause; and while they grasp their swords, can look up to heaven for assistance. Your adversaries are composed of wretches who laugh at the rights of humanity, who turn religion into derision, and would for higher wages direct their swords against their leaders or their country. Go on then, in your generous enterprise, with gratitude to heaven for past success and confidence of it in the future. For my own part, I ask no greater blessing than to share with you the common danger and common glory. If I have a wish dearer to my soul than that my ashes may be mingled with those of a Warren or a Montgomery, it is that these American States may never cease to be *free and independent!*

A Plea for Free Speech in Boston

Frederick Douglass

Frederick Douglass was one of the most famous African-American orators of the nineteenth century. After escaping from his master, this runaway slave fled north where the abolitionist movement was gaining exposure for its efforts to end American slavery. Douglass's talent for public speaking was quickly recognized, and he was hired by the Massachusetts Anti-Slavery Society as a traveling lecturer. In the ensuing years, Douglass became an important orator and writer and spent his life working for the emancipation of slaves as well as for women's rights and free education.

In the following speech, Douglass addresses the hypocrisy of a system of government that prides itself on being founded on the ideals of liberty and free speech and yet extends those rights only to white men. Freedom, he argues, is a universal right—not a selective privilege to be bestowed upon some people and not others. Speaking in Boston in 1860, nearly a century after the spirited debates over liberty that had reverberated through every meeting hall in the city, Douglass makes a plea for free speech for all people, irrespective of race, class, or gender.

An anti-slavery meeting had been recently broken up on the orders of the local government, and Douglass questions why certain people are free to speak out in defense of slavery, while those who oppose slavery are condemned to silence. He answers his own question by arguing that slavery is a tyrannical system, and free speech is a threat to tyranny because it carries the force of truth.

From Frederick Douglass, "A Plea for Free Speech in Boston," delivered in Music Hall, Boston, Massachusetts, 1860, and recorded in *The Liberator*, December 4, 1860, as reprinted in *The World's Best Orations*, edited by David J. Brewer (Chicago: Ferd. P. Kaiser, 1923).

Therefore, supporters of slavery know they must suppress free speech. Indeed, it was for this very reason that the southern states assiduously prevented the northern abolitionists from giving lectures and holding meetings throughout the South.

Boston is a great city—and Music Hall has a fame almost as extensive as that of Boston. Nowhere more than here have the principles of human freedom been expounded. But for the circumstances already mentioned, it would seem almost presumption for me to say anything here about those principles. And yet, even here, in Boston, the moral atmosphere is dark and heavy. The principles of human liberty, even if correctly apprehended, find but limited support in this hour of trial. The world moves slowly, and Boston is much like the world. We thought the principle of free speech was an accomplished fact. Here, if nowhere else, we thought the right of the people to assemble and to express their opinion was secure. Dr. [William] Channing had defended the right, Mr. [William Lloyd] Garrison had practically asserted the right, and Theodore Parker had maintained it with steadiness and fidelity to the last. [Channing, Garrison, and Parker were American abolitionists fighting for the end of slavery.]

But here we are to-day contending for what we thought was gained years ago. The mortifying and disgraceful fact stares us in the face, that though Faneuil Hall and Bunker Hill Monument stand, freedom of speech is struck down. No lengthy detail of facts is needed. They are already notorious; far more so than will be wished ten years hence.

The world knows that last Monday a meeting assembled to discuss the question: "How Shall Slavery Be Abolished?" The world also knows that that meeting was invaded, insulted, captured, by a mob of gentlemen, and thereafter broken up and dispersed by the order of the mayor, who refused to protect it, though called upon to do so. If this had been a mere outbreak of passion and prejudice among the baser sort, maddened by rum and hounded on by some wily politician to serve some immediate purpose,—a mere exceptional affair,—

it might be allowed to rest with what has already been said. But the leaders of the mob were gentlemen. They were men who pride themselves upon their respect for law and order.

These gentlemen brought their respect for the law with them and proclaimed it loudly while in the very act of breaking the law. Theirs was the law of slavery. The law of free speech and the law for the protection of public meetings they trampled under foot, while they greatly magnified the law of slavery.

The scene was an instructive one. Men seldom see such a blending of the gentleman with the rowdy, as was shown on that occasion. It proved that human nature is very much the same, whether in tarpaulin or broadcloth. Nevertheless, when gentlemen approach us in the character of lawless and abandoned loafers,—assuming for the moment their manners and tempers,—they have themselves to blame if they are estimated below their quality.

Freedom of Speech Is Fundamental to Liberty

No right was deemed by the fathers of the Government more sacred than the right of speech. It was in their eyes, as in the eyes of all thoughtful men, the great moral renovator of society and government. Daniel Webster [American statesman] called it a homebred right, a fireside privilege. Liberty is meaningless where the right to utter one's thoughts and opinions has ceased to exist. That, of all rights, is the dread of tyrants. It is the right which they first of all strike down. They know its power. Thrones, dominions, principalities, and powers, founded in injustice and wrong, are sure to tremble, if men are allowed to reason of righteousness, temperance, and of a judgment to come in their presence. Slavery cannot tolerate free speech. Five years of its exercise would banish the auction block and break every chain in the South. They will have none of it there, for they have the power. But shall it be so here?

Even here in Boston, and among the friends of freedom, we hear two voices: one denouncing the mob that broke up our meeting on Monday as a base and cowardly outrage; and another, deprecating and regretting the holding of such a meeting, by such men, at such a time. We are told that the meeting was ill-timed, and the parties to it unwise.

Why, what is the matter with us? Are we going to palliate and excuse a palpable and flagrant outrage on the right of speech by implying that only a particular description of persons should exercise that right? Are we, at such a time, when a great principle has been struck down, to quench the moral indignation which the deed excites, by casting reflections upon those on whose persons the outrage has been committed? After all the arguments for liberty to which Boston has listened for more than a quarter of a century, has she yet to learn that the time to assert a right is the time when the right itself is called in question, and that the men of all others to assert it are the men to whom the right has been denied?

It would be no vindication of the right of speech to prove that certain gentlemen of great distinction, eminent for their learning and ability, are allowed to freely express their opinions on all subjects—including the subject of slavery. Such a vindication would need, itself, to be vindicated. It would add insult to injury. Not even an old-fashioned abolition meeting could vindicate that right in Boston just now. There can be no right of speech where any man, however lifted up, or however humble, however young, or however old, is overawed by force, and compelled to suppress his honest sentiments.

Equally clear is the right to hear. To suppress free speech is a double wrong. It violates the rights of the hearer as well as those of the speaker. It is just as criminal to rob a man of his right to speak and hear as it would be to rob him of his money. I have no doubt that Boston will vindicate this right. But in order to do so, there must be no concessions to the enemy. When a man is allowed to speak because he is rich and powerful, it aggravates the crime of denying the right to the poor and humble.

The principle must rest upon its own proper basis. And until the right is accorded to the humblest as freely as to the most exalted citizen, the government of Boston is but an empty name, and its freedom a mockery. A man's right to speak does not depend upon where he was born or upon his color. The simple quality of manhood is the solid basis of the right—and there let it rest forever.

GREAT
SPEECHES
IN
HISTORY

Debating the Constitution

The Need for a National Government

Benjamin Franklin

When Benjamin Franklin delivered the following speech
at the Constitutional Convention in Philadelphia in 1787,
it was at the end of a career in public life that had
spanned nearly six decades. At eighty-one, Franklin was
adored by the American public; for many people,
Franklin's support of the controversial new Constitution
(along with George Washington's) stamped the endeavor
with a mark of approval.

The Philadelphia Convention, which convened in
1787 in order to amend the Articles of Confederation,
ended up exceeding its initial charter and creating a Constitution that contrasted markedly with its predecessor.
The Articles that had been drawn up in 1777 created a
loose organization more akin to a treaty among independent sovereign states than the charter of a single country.
The inability of the national governing body to tax individuals in a time of severe economic depression, combined with the fear of insurrections such as the recent rebellion led by Daniel Shays, persuaded certain men like
Alexander Hamilton, James Madison, and Benjamin
Franklin of the need for a strong, centralized government
with the powers to supersede individual states' claims.

Yet others, most notably Patrick Henry and a strong
Virginian contingent, feared the potential for the abuse of
power that was believed to be inherent in the notion of
national government. While Henry himself completely

From Benjamin Franklin, "On the Federal Constitution," delivered at the Consti-
tutional Convention, Philadelphia, Pennsylvania, 1787, as reprinted in *The
World's Famous Orations*, vol. 8, edited by William Jennings Bryan (New York:
Funk Wagnalls, 1906).

boycotted the Virginia convention, other "localists" like
him argued for months against the very concept of a national Constitution. There were major issues that needed
to be decided, including how many houses the government was to have, how representatives were to be elected,
how the states were to be represented (by one vote each
or by representatives proportional to their population),
and whether slaves were to be included in the population
count. There was general consensus on the necessity of
separating power among the various branches of government, yet it was unclear how this was to be effected.

Over the course of several months, many compromises were made and many solutions were finally
reached. A tripartite system of government was decided
upon, with executive, legislative, and judicial branches
that were to serve as a system of checks and balances for
one another and that were to have differing and staggered terms of appointment for their officials. Modeled
on the British Houses of Lords and Commons, the legislative wing was to have a Senate in which each state
had two representatives along with a House of Representatives, whose members would be elected in numbers proportional to each state's population, making this body
more sensitive to popular opinion.

In the following speech, Franklin suggests that the
Constitution is essentially a document of compromise
that reflects a willingness to overcome dogmatism and
partisan interests. Franklin reiterates the exigency of a
national constitution and urges a united support of the
document especially in the international arena, whatever
flaws some might believe it to have. Finally, Franklin expresses pride in the unity and spirit of cooperation that
had produced the Constitution, announcing that he
thinks it will astonish America's enemies.

I confess that I do not entirely approve of this Constitution
at present; but, sir, I am not sure I shall never approve of
it, for, having lived long, I have experienced many in-

stances of being obliged, by better information or fuller consideration, to change opinions even on important subjects, which I once thought right, but found to be otherwise. It is therefore that, the older I grow, the more apt I am to doubt my own judgment of others. Most men, indeed, as well as most sects in religion, think themselves in possession of all truth, and that wherever others differ from them, it is so far error. Steele, a Protestant, in a dedication, tells the pope that the only

Benjamin Franklin

difference between our two churches in their opinions of the certainty of their doctrine is, the Romish Church is infallible, and the Church of England is never in the wrong. But, tho many private persons think almost as highly of their own infallibility as of that of their sect, few express it so naturally as a certain French lady, who, in a little dispute with her sister, said: "But I meet with nobody but myself that is always in the right."

In these sentiments, sir, I agree to this Constitution with all its faults—if they are such—because I think a general government necessary for us, and there is no form of government but what may be a blessing to the people if well administered; and I believe, further, that this is likely to be well administered for a course of years, and can only end in despotism, as other forms have done before it, when the people shall become so corrupted as to need despotic government, being incapable of any other. I doubt, too, whether any other convention we can obtain may be able to make a better Constitution; for, when you assemble a number of men, to have the advantage of their joint wisdom, you inevitably assemble with those men all their prejudices, their passions, their errors of opinion, their local interests, and their selfish views. From such an assembly can a perfect production be expected?

It therefore astonishes me, sir, to find this system approaching so near to perfection as it does; and I think it will astonish our enemies, who are waiting with confidence to hear that our counsels are confounded like those of the builders of Babel, and that our States are on the point of separation, only to meet hereafter for the purpose of cutting one another's throats. Thus I consent, sir, to this Constitution, because I expect no better, and because I am not sure that it is not the best. The opinions I have had of its errors I sacrifice to the public good. I have never whispered a syllable of them abroad. Within these walls they were born, and here they shall die. If every one of us, in returning to our constituents, were to report the objections he has had to it, and endeavor to gain partizans in support of them, we might prevent its being generally received, and thereby lose all the salutary effects and great advantages resulting naturally in our favor among foreign nations, as well as among ourselves, from our real or apparent unanimity. Much of the strength and efficiency of any government, in procuring and securing happiness to the people, depends on opinion, on the general opinion of the goodness of that government, as well as of the wisdom and integrity of its governors. I hope, therefore, for our own sakes, as a part of the people, and for the sake of our posterity, that we shall act heartily and unanimously in recommending this Constitution wherever our influence may extend, and turn our future thoughts and endeavors to the means of having it well administered.

On the whole, sir, I can not help expressing a wish that every member of the convention who may still have objections to it, would, with me, on this occasion, doubt a little of his own infallibility, and, to make manifest our unanimity, put his name to this instrument.

Against the Federal Constitution

Patrick Henry

The delegates to the Constitutional Convention in Philadelphia had worked in secrecy throughout the long, hot summer and into the fall of 1787. Eventually, the Constitution was complete: The delegates had discussed every angle they could think of, pored over each word, and debated each phrase until finally they had reached consensus. The delegates' jobs were now done, and it was time for the states to approve the Constitution by ratifying it. For more than a year, furious debates ensued within the state legislatures, as the Federalists (those supporting the Constitution and the creation of a strong national government) and the Anti-Federalists (those opposing the Constitution) battled out their vision of the new America.

Delaware, Pennsylvania, and New Jersey were quick to ratify the Constitution in 1787, and several more states followed in 1788. However, the debate in Virginia was particularly long and drawn out. Virginia was seen as an especially important state, partly due to its size and influence, and partly because many hoped it would be the essential ninth state to ratify (nine states had to ratify for the Constitution to become effective). In the following speech made in June 1788, Patrick Henry, former governor and longtime member of the Virginia legislature, passionately opposes ratification.

The newly penned Constitution limited the individual states' power and relocated the powers of direct taxing and military authority to a national authority. Henry was suspicious of a strong, centralized government for its

From Patrick Henry, "Against the Federal Constitution," delivered at the Virginia Ratification Convention, Richmond, Virginia, June 5, 1788, as reprinted in *Select Orations Illustrating American Political History*, edited by Samuel Bannister Harding (New York: Macmillan, 1909).

proximity to the monarchical British model that had so
recently proved itself a system that invited abuses of
power. He feared that the powerful executive office envisioned for the president would reinstitute a tyrannical
kinglike figure. Furthermore, Virginia was one of the
largest and most powerful states, and Henry was concerned that state interests would be constantly foiled by
the divergent interests of tiny states such as Rhode Island.
But most of all, Henry claimed that he feared for "American liberty," imagining that the most pessimistic conceiv-
able scenarios for the abuse of power lay embedded in
the Constitution.

Henry attacked the Constitution by revealing its
lacks and omissions and by citing potential problems. His
objections were thus mostly in the form of negatives. Yet
he failed to present a viable alternative to the Articles of
Confederation, which everybody admitted to be deeply
flawed. Thus lacking a better solution, those opposing
the Constitution eventually conceded, and Virginia ratified the Constitution in June 1788.

I rose yesterday to ask a question ["What right had they to
say, 'We, the people,' instead of 'We, the States'?"], which
arose in my own mind. When I asked that question, I
thought the meaning of my interrogation was obvious: the
fate of this question and of America may depend on this.
Have they said, "We, the States"? Have they made a proposal of a compact between States? If they had, this would be
a confederation: it is otherwise most clearly a consolidated
government. The question turns, sir, on that poor little
thing—the expression, "We, the *people*," instead of, "the
States" of America. I need not take much pains to show, that
the principles of this system are extremely pernicious, impolitic, and dangerous. Is this a monarchy, like England—a
compact between prince and people; with checks on the former to secure the liberty of the latter? Is this a confederacy,
like Holland—an association of a number of independent
states, each of which retains its individual sovereignty? It is

not a democracy, wherein the people retain all their rights securely. Had these principles been adhered to, we should not
have been brought to this alarming transition, from a confederacy to a consolidated government. We have no detail of
those great considerations which, in my opinion, ought to
have abounded before we should recur to a government of
this kind. Here is a revolution as radical as that which separated us from Great Britain. It is as radical, if in this transition our rights and privileges are endangered, and the sovereignty of the States relinquished: and can not we plainly see
that this is actually the case? The rights of conscience, trial
by jury, liberty of the press, all your immunities and fran-
chises, all pretensions to human rights and privileges, are rendered insecure if not lost, by this change so loudly talked of
by some and inconsiderately by others. Is this tame relinquishment of rights worthy of freemen? Is it worthy of that
manly fortitude that ought to characterize republicans? It is
said eight States have adopted this plan. I declare that if
twelve States and an half had adopted it, I would, with manly
firmness and in spite of an erring world, reject it. You are not
to inquire how your trade may be increased, nor how you are
to become a great and powerful people, but how your liberties can be secured; for liberty ought to be the direct end of
your government.

We Must Guard Liberty

Having premised these things, I shall, with the aid of my
judgment and information, which I confess are not extensive,
go into the discussion of this system more minutely. Is it necessary for your liberty, that you should abandon those great
rights by the adoption of this system? Is the relinquishment
of the trial by jury, and the liberty of the press, necessary for
your liberty? Will the abandonment of your most sacred
rights tend to the security of your liberty? Liberty, the greatest of all earthly blessings—give us that precious jewel, and
you may take everything else! . . . Guard with jealous attention the public liberty. Suspect every one who approaches
that jewel. Unfortunately, nothing will preserve it but down-
right force. Whenever you give up that force, you are in-

evitably ruined. I am answered by gentlemen that, though I may speak of terrors, yet the fact is that we are surrounded by none of the dangers I apprehend. I conceive this new government to be one of those dangers: it has produced those horrors which distress many of our best citizens. We are come hither to preserve the poor commonwealth of Virginia, if it can be possibly done: something must be done to preserve your liberty and mine. The Confederation, this same despised government, merits in my opinion the highest encomium: it carried us through a long and dangerous war; it rendered us victorious in that bloody conflict with a powerful nation; it has secured us a territory greater than any European monarch possesses; and shall a government which has been thus strong and vigorous be accused of imbecility, and abandoned for want of energy? Consider what you are about to do, before you part with this government. Take longer time in reckoning things: revolutions like this have happened in almost every country in Europe: similar examples are to be found in ancient Greece and ancient Rome—instances of the people losing their liberty by their own carelessness and the ambition of a few. We are cautioned by the honorable gentleman who presides [Edmund Pendleton] against faction and turbulence. I acknowledge that licentiousness is dangerous, and that it ought to be provided against: I acknowledge also the new form of government may effectually prevent it: yet there is another thing it will as effectually do—it will oppress and ruin the people.

The Danger of Tyranny

There are sufficient guards placed against sedition and licentiousness; for when power is given to this government to suppress these, or for any other purpose, the language it assumes is clear, express and unequivocal; but when this Constitution speaks of privileges, there is an ambiguity, sir, a fatal ambiguity—an ambiguity which is very astonishing. In the clause under consideration, there is the strangest language that I can conceive. I mean when it says, that there shall not be more representatives than one for every 30,000. Now, sir, how easy is it to evade this privilege? "The number shall not exceed one for every 30,000." This may be satisfied by one representative from each State. Let our numbers be ever so great, this immense continent may, by this artful expression, be reduced to have but thirteen representatives. I confess this construction is not natural; but the ambiguity of the expression lays a good ground for a quarrel. . . . This possibility of reducing the number to one for each State approximates to probability by that other expression, "but each State shall at least have one representative." . . . I shall be told I am continually afraid: but, sir, I have strong cause of apprehension. In some parts of the plan before you, the great rights of freemen are endangered, in other parts absolutely taken away. How does your trial by jury stand? In civil cases gone—not sufficiently secured in criminal—this best privilege is gone. But we are told that we need not fear because those in power, being our representatives, will not abuse the powers we put in their hands. I am not well versed in history; but I will submit to your recollection, whether liberty has been destroyed most often by the licentiousness of the people, or by the tyranny of rulers. I imagine, sir, you will find the balance on the side of tyranny. . . . My great objection to this government is, that it does not leave us the means of defending our rights, or of waging war against tyrants. It is urged by some gentlemen, that this new plan will bring us an acquisition of strength—an army, and the militia of the States. This is an idea extremely ridiculous: gentlemen can not be in earnest. This acquisition will trample on our fallen liberty. Let my beloved Americans guard against that fatal lethargy that has pervaded the universe. Have we the means of resisting disciplined armies, when our only defense, the militia, is put into the hands of Congress? . . .

Amendments Will Not Be Easy

To encourage us to adopt it [the Constitution], they tell us that there is a plain easy way of getting amendments. When I come to contemplate this part, I suppose that I am mad, or that my countrymen are so. The way to amendment is, in my conception, shut. Let us consider this plain easy way. "The Congress, whenever two-thirds of both houses shall deem it necessary, shall propose amendments to this Constitution; or, on the application of the legislatures of two-thirds of the several States, shall call a convention for proposing amendments, which, in either case, shall be valid to all intents and purposes, as part of this Constitution, when ratified by the legislatures of three-fourths of the several States, or by conventions in three-fourths thereof, as the one or the other mode of ratification may be proposed by the Congress. . . ." Hence it appears that three-fourths of the States must ultimately agree to any amendments that may be necessary. Let us consider the consequences of this. However uncharitable it may appear, yet I must express my opinion—that the most unworthy characters may get into power and prevent the introduction of amendments. Let us suppose (for the case is supposable, possible, and probable), that you happen to deal these powers to unworthy hands; will they relinquish powers already in their possession, or agree to amendments? Two-thirds of the Congress, or of the State legislatures, are necessary even to propose amendments. If one-third of these be unworthy men, they may prevent the application for amendments; but what is destructive and mischievous is, that three-fourths of the State legislatures, or of the State conventions, must concur in the amendments when proposed! In such numerous bodies, there must necessarily be some designing, bad men. To suppose that so large a number as three-fourths of the States will concur, is to suppose that they will possess genius, intelligence, and integrity, approaching to miraculous. It would, indeed, be miraculous, that they should concur in the same amendments, or even in such as would bear some likeness to one another. For four of the smallest States, that do not collectively contain one-tenth part of the population of the United States, may obstruct the most salutary and necessary amendments. Nay, in these four States, six-tenths of the people may reject these amendments; and suppose that amendments shall be opposed to amendments (which is highly probable), is it possible that three-fourths can ever agree to the same amendments? A bare majority in these four small States may hinder the adoption of amendments; so that we may fairly and justly conclude, that one-twentieth part of the American people may prevent the removal of the most grievous inconveniences and oppression, by refusing to accede to amendments. A trifling minority may reject the most salutary amendments. Is this an easy mode of securing the public liberty? It is, sir, a most fearful situation, when the most contemptible minority can prevent the alteration of the most oppressive government; for it may, in many respects, prove to be such. Is this the spirit of republicanism? . . . This, sir, is the language of democracy—that a majority of the community have a right to alter their government when found to be oppressive. But how different is the genius of your new Constitution from this! How different from the sentiments of freemen, that a contemptible minority can prevent the good of the majority! . . .

The States Will Have No Power

Let us here call your attention to that part which gives the Congress power "to provide for organizing, arming, and disciplining the militia, and for governing such part of them as may be employed in the service of the United States—reserving to the States respectively the appointment of the officers, and the authority of training the militia, according to the discipline prescribed by Congress." By this, sir, you see that their control over our last and best defense is unlimited. If they neglect or refuse to discipline or arm our militia, they will be useless: the States can do neither, this power being exclusively given to Congress. The power of appointing officers over men not disciplined or armed is ridiculous; so that this pretended little remnant of power left to the States may, at the pleasure of Congress, be rendered nugatory. Our situation will be deplorable indeed: nor can we ever expect to get this government amended; since I have already shown that a very small minority may prevent it, and that small minority interested in the continuance of the oppression. Will the oppressor let go the oppressed? Was there ever an instance? Can the annals of mankind exhibit one single example where rulers, overcharged with power, willingly let go the oppressed, though solicited and requested most earnestly? The application for amendments will therefore be fruitless. Sometimes the oppressed have got loose by one of those bloody

struggles that desolate a country; but a willing relinquishment of power is one of those things which human nature
never was, nor ever will be, capable of. . . .

State Interests Will Be Blocked

I have said that I thought this a consolidated government: I
will now prove it. Will the great rights of the people be secured by this government? Suppose it should prove oppressive; how can it be altered? Our Bill of Rights declares, "that
a majority of the community hath an indubitable, unalienable,
and indefeasible right to reform, alter or abolish it, in such
manner as shall be judged most conducive to the public weal."
I have just proved, that one-tenth, or less, of the people of
America—a most despicable minority—may prevent this reform, or alteration. Suppose the people of Virginia should
wish to alter their government; can a majority of them do it?
No, because they are connected with other men; or, in other
words, consolidated with other States. When the people of
Virginia, at a future day, shall wish to alter their government,
though they should be unanimous in this desire, yet they may
be prevented therefrom by a despicable minority at the extremity of the United States. The founders of your own constitution made your government changeable; but the power of
changing it is gone from you! Whither is it gone? It is placed
in the same hands that hold the rights of twelve other States;
and those who hold those rights have right and power to keep
them. It is not the particular government of Virginia: one of
the leading features of that government is, that a majority can
alter it, when necessary for the public good. This government
is not a Virginian, but an American government. Is it not
therefore a consolidated government? The sixth clause of your
Bill of Rights tells you, "that elections of members to serve as
representatives of the people in assembly, ought to be free, and
that all men having sufficient evidence of permanent common
interest with and attachment to the community, have the right
of suffrage, and can not be *taxed* or deprived of their property
for public uses, without their own consent, or that of their
representatives so elected, nor bound by any law to which
they have not in like manner assented for the public good."

But what does this Constitution say? The clause under consideration gives an unlimited and unbounded power of taxation. Suppose every delegate from Virginia opposes a law laying a tax; what will it avail? They are opposed by a majority: eleven members can destroy their efforts: those feeble ten cannot prevent the passing the most oppressive tax-law; so that, in direct opposition to the spirit and express language of your declaration of rights, you are taxed, not by your own consent, but by people who have no connection with you. . . .

A President Like a King?

This Constitution can counteract and suspend any of our laws, that contravene its oppressive operation; for they have the power of direct taxation, which suspends our Bill of Rights; and it is expressly provided, that they can make all laws necessary for carrying their powers into execution; and it is declared paramount to the laws and constitutions of the States. Consider how the only remaining defense we have left is destroyed in this manner. Besides the expenses of maintaining the Senate and other house in as much splendor as they please, there is to be a great and mighty president, with very extensive powers—the powers of a king. He is to be supported in extravagant magnificence; so that the whole of our property may be taken by this American government, by laying what taxes they please, giving themselves what salaries they please, and suspending our laws at their pleasure. I might be thought too inquisitive, but I believe I should take up but very little of your time in enumerating the little power that is left to the government of Virginia; for this power is reduced to little or nothing. Their garrisons, magazines, arsenals, and forts, which will be situated in the strongest places within the States,—their ten miles square, with all the fine ornaments of human life, added to their powers, and taken from the States, will reduce the power of the latter to nothing. . . .

Elections

What can be more defective than the clause concerning the elections? The control given to Congress over the time, place, and manner of holding elections, will totally destroy the end of suffrage. The elections may be held at one place, and the most inconvenient in the State; or they may be at remote distances from those who have a right of suffrage: hence nine out of ten must either not vote at all, or vote for strangers; for the most influential characters will be applied to, to know who are the most proper to be chosen. I repeat, that the control of Congress over the *manner*, etc., of electing, well warrants this idea. The natural consequence will be, that this democratic branch will possess none of the public confidence; the people will be prejudiced against representatives chosen in such an injudicious manner. The proceedings in the northern conclave will be hidden from the yeomanry of this country. We are told that the yeas and nays shall be taken and entered on the journal. This, sir, will avail nothing: it may be locked up in their chests, and concealed forever from the people; for they are not to publish what parts they think require secrecy: they *may* think, and *will* think, the whole requires it.

Where Does Responsibility Lie?

Another beautiful feature of this Constitution is the publication, from time to time, of the receipts and expenditures of the public money. This expression, *from time to time,* is very indefinite and indeterminate: it may extend to a century. Grant that any of them are wicked; they may squander the public money so as to ruin you, and yet this expression will give you no redress. I say, they may ruin you; for where, sir, is the responsibility? The yeas and nays will show you nothing, unless they be fools as well as knaves; for, after having wickedly trampled on the rights of the people, they would act like fools indeed were they to publish and divulge their iniquity, when they have it equally in their power to suppress and conceal it. Where is the responsibility—that leading principle in the British government? In that government, a punishment, certain and inevitable, is provided; but in this there is no real, actual punishment for the grossest mal-administration. They may go without punishment, though they commit the most outrageous violation on our immunities. That paper may tell me they will be punished. I ask, By what law? They must make the law, for there is no existing law to do it. What! will they make a law to punish themselves?

This, sir, is my great objection to the Constitution, that there is no true responsibility, and that the preservation of our liberty depends on the single chance of men being virtuous enough to make laws to punish themselves. In the country from which we are descended, they have real, and not imaginary responsibility; for there mal-administration has cost their heads to some of the most saucy geniuses that ever were. The Senate, by making treaties, may destroy your liberty and laws for want of responsibility. Two-thirds of those that shall happen to be present can, with the President, make treaties that shall be the supreme law of the land: they may make the most ruinous treaties, and yet there is no punishment for them. Whoever shows me a punishment provided for them will oblige me.

We Must Reject This Constitution

So, sir, notwithstanding there are eight pillars, they want another. Where will they make another? I trust, sir, the exclusion of the evils wherewith this system is replete, in its present form, will be made a condition precedent to its adoption, by this or any other State.

For the Federal Constitution

James Madison

On June 6, 1788, the day after Patrick Henry spoke out in opposition to ratifying the Constitution, James Madison, one of the most eloquent defenders of the document, rebutted the aging Virginian's concerns. Madison was well versed in the constitutional debates, having been a key figure at the Constitutional Convention in Philadelphia in 1787 where the document had been drawn up; in fact, the first article of the Constitution was based on the Virginia Plan that Madison had authored. During the ensuing months of debate, James Madison, John Jay, and Alexander Hamilton had also written a collection of essays defending the Constitution (*The Federalist Papers*), which had appeared in weekly columns in the New York newspapers in order to garner Federalist support in that sharply divided state.

In the following excerpts, Madison emphasizes the system of power checks among the three branches, while noting that there is little chance of tyranny due to the presence of many divergent interests which make it difficult for one group to gain control. He also stresses the importance of a national taxing authority to deal effectively with America's current postwar economic crisis. Finally, he argues that the Constitution is fair because it allows for proportional representation, giving larger, more populous states greater representation in the House.

The Virginia Federalists led by Madison ultimately won the debate. After several more weeks of debate, and after securing promises of forthcoming amendments to

From James Madison, "For the Federal Constitution," delivered at the Virginia Ratification Convention, Richmond, Virginia, June 6, 1788, as reprinted in *American Forum: Speeches on Historic Issues, 1788–1900*, edited by Ernest J. Wrage and Barnet Baskerville (New York: Harper & Brothers, 1960).

protect human rights (the Bill of Rights), Virginia ratified in late June. By this time, however, New Hampshire had become the pivotal ninth state needed to put the Constitution into effect.

Before I proceed to make some additions to the reasons which have been adduced by my honorable friend over the way, I must take the liberty to make some observations on what was said by another gentleman [Mr. Patrick Henry]. He told us that this Constitution ought to be rejected because it endangered the public liberty, in his opinion, in many instances. Give me leave to make one answer to that observation: Let the dangers which this system is supposed to be replete with be clearly pointed out: if any dangerous and unnecessary powers be given to the general legislature, let them be plainly demonstrated; and let us not rest satisfied with general assertions of danger, without examination. If powers be necessary, apparent danger is not a sufficient reason against conceding them. He has suggested that licentiousness has seldom produced the loss of liberty; but that the tyranny of rulers has almost always effected it. Since the general civilization of mankind, I believe there are more instances of the abridgment of the freedom of the people by gradual and silent encroachments of those in power, than by violent and sudden usurpations; but, on a candid examination of history, we shall find that turbulence, violence, and abuse of power, by the majority trampling on the rights of the minority, have produced factions and commotions, which, in republics, have, more frequently than any other cause, produced despotism. If we go over the whole history of ancient and modern republics, we shall find their destruction to have generally resulted from those causes. If we consider the peculiar situation of the United States, and what are the sources of that diversity of sentiment which pervades its inhabitants, we shall find great danger to fear that the same causes may terminate here in the same fatal effects which they produced in those republics. This danger ought to be wisely guarded against. Perhaps, in the progress of this discussion, it will appear that the only possible remedy for those evils, and means of preserving and protecting the principles of republicanism, will be found in that very system which is now exclaimed against as the parent of oppression.

Inconsistent Arguments

I must confess I have not been able to find his usual consistency in the gentleman's argument on this occasion. He informs us that the people of the country are at perfect repose,— that is, every man enjoys the fruits of his labor peaceably and securely, and that every thing is in perfect tranquillity and safety. I wish sincerely, sir, this were true. If this be their happy situation, why has every state acknowledged the contrary? Why were deputies from all the states sent to the general Convention? Why have complaints of national and individual distresses been echoed and reechoed throughout the continent? Why has our general government been so shamefully disgraced, and our Constitution violated? Wherefore have laws been made to authorize a change, and wherefore are we now assembled here? A federal government is formed for the protection of its individual members. Ours has attacked itself with impunity. Its authority has been disobeyed and despised. I think I perceive a glaring inconsistency in another of his arguments. He complains of this Constitution, because it requires the consent of at least three fourths of the states to introduce amendments which shall be necessary for the happiness of the people. The assent of so many he urges as too great an obstacle to the admission of salutary amendments, which, he strongly insists, ought to be at the will of a bare majority. We hear this argument, at the very moment we are called upon to assign reasons for proposing a constitution which puts it in the power of nine states to abolish the present inadequate, unsafe, and pernicious Confederation! In the first case, he asserts that a majority ought to have the power of altering the government, when found to be inadequate to the security of public happiness. In the last case, he affirms that even three fourths of the community have not a right to alter a government which experience has proved to be subversive of national felicity! nay, that the most necessary and urgent alterations cannot be made without the absolute unanimity of all the states! Does not the thirteenth article of the Confederation expressly require that no alteration shall be made without the unanimous consent of all the states? Could any thing in theory be more perniciously improvident and injudicious than this submission of the will of the majority to the most trifling minority? Have not experience and practice actually manifested this theoretical inconvenience to be extremely impolitic? Let me mention one fact, which I conceive must carry conviction to the mind of any one: the smallest state in the Union has obstructed every attempt to reform the government; that little member has repeatedly disobeyed and counteracted the general authority; nay, has even supplied the enemies of its country with provisions. Twelve states had agreed to certain improvements which were proposed, being thought absolutely necessary to preserve the existence of the general government; but as these improvements, though really indispensable, could not, by the Confederation, be introduced into it without the consent of every state, the refractory dissent of that little state prevented their adoption. The inconveniences resulting from this requisition, of unanimous concurrence in alterations in the Confederation, must be known to every member in this Convention; it is therefore needless to remind them of them. Is it not self-evident that a trifling minority ought not to bind the majority? Would not foreign influence be exerted with facility over a small minority? Would the honorable gentleman agree to continue the most radical defects in the old system, because the petty state of Rhode Island would not agree to remove them?

Seat of Government and the Militia

He next objects to the exclusive legislation over the district where the seat of government may be fixed. Would he submit that the representatives of this state should carry on their deliberations under the control of any other member of the Union? If any state had the power of legislation over the place where Congress should fix the general government, this would impair the dignity, and hazard the safety, of Congress.

If the safety of the Union were under the control of any particular state, would not foreign corruption probably prevail, in such a state, to induce it to exert its controlling influence over the members of the general government? . . . When we also reflect that the previous cession of particular states is necessary before Congress can legislate exclusively any where, we must, instead of being alarmed at this part, heartily approve of it.

But the honorable member sees great danger in the provision concerning the militia. This I conceive to be an additional security to our liberty, without diminishing the power of the states in any considerable degree. It appears to me so highly expedient that I should imagine it would have found advocates even in the warmest friends of the present system. The authority of training the militia, and appointing the officers, is reserved to the states. Congress ought to have the power to establish a uniform discipline throughout the states, and to provide for the execution of the laws, suppress insurrections, and repel invasions: these are the only cases wherein they can interfere with the militia; and the obvious necessity of their having power over them in these cases must convince any reflecting mind. Without uniformity of discipline, military bodies would be incapable of action: without a general controlling power to call forth the strength of the Union to repel invasions, the country might be overrun and conquered by foreign enemies: without such a power to suppress insurrections, our liberties might be destroyed by domestic faction, and domestic tyranny be established.

The honorable member then told us that there was no instance of power once transferred being voluntarily renounced. Not to produce European examples, which may probably be done before the rising of this Convention, have we not seen already, in seven states (and probably in an eighth state), legislatures surrendering some of the most important powers they possessed? But, sir, by this government, powers are not given to any particular set of men; they are in the hands of the people; delegated to their representatives chosen for short terms; to representatives responsible to the people, and whose situation is perfectly similar to their own. As long as this is the case we have no danger to apprehend.

When the gentleman called our recollection to the usual effects of the concession of powers, and imputed the loss of liberty generally to open tyranny, I wish he had gone on farther. Upon his review of history, he would have found that the loss of liberty very often resulted from factions and divisions; from local considerations, which eternally lead to quarrels; he would have found internal dissensions to have more frequently demolished civil liberty, than a tenacious disposition in rulers to retain any stipulated powers. . . .

The power of raising and supporting armies is exclaimed against as dangerous and unnecessary. I wish there were no necessity of vesting this power in the general government. But suppose a foreign nation to declare war against the United States; must not the general legislature have the power of defending the United States? Ought it to be known to foreign nations that the general government of the United States of America has no power to raise and support an army, even in the utmost danger, when attacked by external ene-

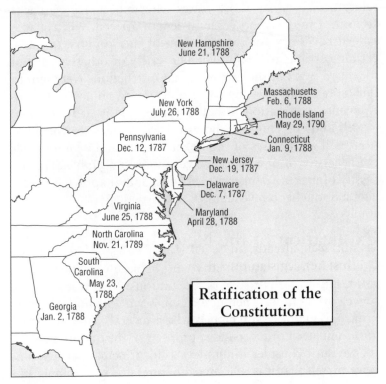

New Hampshire
June 21, 1788

New York
July 26, 1788

Massachusetts
Feb. 6, 1788

Rhode Island
May 29, 1790

Pennsylvania
Dec. 12, 1787

Connecticut
Jan. 9, 1788

New Jersey
Dec. 19, 1787

Delaware
Dec. 7, 1787

Virginia
June 25, 1788

Maryland
April 28, 1788

North Carolina
Nov. 21, 1789

South
Carolina
May 23,
1788

Georgia
Jan. 2, 1788

Ratification of the Constitution

mies? Would not their knowledge of such a circumstance stimulate them to fall upon us? If, sir, Congress be not invested with this power, any powerful nation, prompted by ambition or avarice, will be invited, by our weakness, to attack us; and such an attack, by disciplined veterans, would certainly be attended with success, when only opposed by irregular, undisciplined militia. Whoever considers the peculiar situation of this country, the multiplicity of its excellent inlets and harbors, and the uncommon facility of attacking it,—however much he may regret the necessity of such a power, cannot hesitate a moment in granting it. One fact may elucidate this argument. In the course of the late war, when the weak parts of the Union were exposed, and many states were in the most deplorable situation by the enemy's ravages, the assistance of foreign nations was thought so urgently necessary for our protection, that the relinquishment of territorial advantages was not deemed too great a sacrifice for the acquisition of one ally. This expedient was admitted with great reluctance, even by those states who expected advantages from it. The crisis, however, at length arrived, when it was judged necessary for the salvation of this country to make certain cessions to Spain; whether wisely or otherwise is not for me to say; but the fact was, that instructions were sent to our representative at the court of Spain, to empower him to enter into negotiations for that purpose. How it terminated is well known. This fact shows the extremities to which nations will go in cases of imminent danger, and demonstrates the necessity of making ourselves more respectable. The necessity of making dangerous cessions, and of applying to foreign aid, ought to be excluded. . . .

Explication of the New Government

Give me leave to say something of the nature of the government, and to show that it is safe and just to vest it with the power of taxation. There are a number of opinions; but the principal question is, whether it be a federal or consolidated government. In order to judge properly of the question before us, we must consider it minutely in its principal parts. I conceive myself that it is of a mixed nature; it is in a manner unprecedented; we cannot find one express example in the experience of the world. It stands by itself. In some respects it is a government of a federal nature; in others, it is of a consolidated nature. Even if we attend to the manner in which the Constitution is investigated, ratified, and made the act of the people of America, I can say, notwithstanding what the honorable gentleman has alleged, that this government is not completely consolidated, nor is it entirely federal. Who are parties to it? The people—but not the people as composing one great body; but the people as composing thirteen sovereignties. Were it, as the gentleman asserts, a consolidated government, the assent of a majority of the people would be sufficient for its establishment; and, as a majority have adopted it already, the remaining states would be bound by the act of the majority, even if they unanimously reprobated it. Were it such a government as is suggested, it would be now binding on the people of this state, without having had the privilege of deliberating upon it. But, sir, no state is bound by it, as it is, without its own consent. Should all the states adopt it, it will be then a government established by the thirteen states of America, not through the intervention of the legislatures, but by the people at large. In this particular respect, the distinction between the existing and proposed governments is very material. The existing system has been derived from the dependent derivative authority of the legislatures of the states; whereas this is derived from the superior power of the people. If we look at the manner in which alterations are to be made in it, the same idea is, in some degree, attended to. By the new system, a majority of the states cannot introduce amendments; nor are all the states required for that purpose; three fourths of them must concur in alterations; in this there is a departure from the federal idea. The members to the national House of Representatives are to be chosen by the people at large, in proportion to the numbers in the respective districts. When we come to the Senate, its members are elected by the states in their equal and political capacity. But had the government been completely consolidated, the Senate would have been chosen by the people in their individual capacity, in the same manner as the members of the other house. Thus it is of a complicated nature; and this complication, I trust, will be found to exclude the evils of absolute consolidation, as well as of a mere confederacy. If Virginia was separated from all the states, her power and authority would extend to all cases: in like manner, were all powers vested in the general government, it would be a consolidated government; but the powers of the federal government are enumerated; it can only operate in certain cases; it has legislative powers on defined and limited objects, beyond which it cannot extend its jurisdiction.

The Power to Tax

But the honorable member has satirized, with peculiar acrimony, the powers given to the general government by this Constitution. I conceive that the first question on this subject is, whether these powers be necessary; if they be, we are reduced to the dilemma of either submitting to the inconvenience or losing the Union. Let us consider the most important of these reprobated powers; that of direct taxation is most generally objected to. With respect to the exigencies of government, there is no question but the most easy mode of providing for them will be adopted. When, therefore, direct taxes are not necessary, they will not be recurred to. It can be of little advantage to those in power to raise money in a manner oppressive to the people. To consult the conveniences of the people will cost them nothing, and in many respects will be advantageous to them. Direct taxes will only be recurred to for great purposes. What has brought on other nations those immense debts, under the pressure of which many of them labor? Not the expenses of their governments, but war. If this country should be engaged in war,—and I conceive we ought to provide for the possibility of such a case,—how would it be carried on? By the usual means provided from year to year? As our imports will be necessary for the expenses of government and other common exigencies, how are we to carry on the means of defence? How is it possible a war could be supported without money or credit? and would it be possible for a government to have credit without having the power of raising money? No; it would be impossible for any government, in such a case, to defend itself. Then, I say, sir, that it is necessary to establish funds for extraordinary exigencies, and to give this power to the general government; for the utter inutility of previous requisitions on the states is too well known. Would it be possible for those countries, whose finances and revenues are carried to the highest perfection, to carry on the operations of government on great emergencies, such as the maintenance of a war, without an uncontrolled power of raising money? Has it not been necessary for Great Britain, notwithstanding the facility of the collection of her taxes, to have recourse very often to this and other extraordinary methods of procuring money? Would not her public credit have been ruined, if it was known that her power to raise money was limited? Has not France been obliged, on great occasions, to use unusual means to raise funds? It has been the case in many countries, and no government can exist unless its powers extend to make provisions for every contingency. If we were actually attacked by a powerful nation, and our general government had not the power of raising money, but depended solely on requisitions, our condition would be truly deplorable: if the revenue of this commonwealth were to depend on twenty distinct authorities, it would be impossible for it to carry on its operations. This must be obvious to every member here; I think, therefore, that it is necessary, for the preservation of the Union, that this power shall be given to the general government.

But it is urged that its consolidated nature, joined to the power of direct taxation, will give it a tendency to destroy all subordinate authority; that its increasing influence will speedily enable it to absorb the state governments. I cannot think this will be the case. If the general government were wholly independent of the governments of the particular states, then, indeed, usurpation might be expected to the fullest extent. But, sir, on whom does this general government depend? It derives its authority from these governments, and from the same sources from which their authority is derived. The members of the federal government are taken from the same men from whom those of the state legislatures are taken. If we consider the mode in which the federal representatives will be chosen, we shall be convinced that the general will never destroy the individual governments; and this conviction must be strengthened by an attention to the construction of the Senate. The representatives will be chosen probably under the influence of the members of the state legislatures; but there is not the least probability that the election of the latter will be influenced by the former. One hundred and sixty members represent this commonwealth in one branch of the legislature, are drawn from the people at large, and must ever possess more influence than the few men who will be elected to the general legislature. . . .

Those who wish to become federal representatives must depend on their credit with that class of men who will be the most popular in their counties, who generally represent the people in the state governments; they can, therefore, never succeed in any measure contrary to the wishes of those on whom they depend. It is almost certain, therefore, that the deliberations of the members of the federal House of Representatives will be directed to the interest of the people of America. As to the other branch, the senators will be appointed by the legislatures; and, though elected for six years, I do not conceive they will so soon forget the source from whence they derive their political existence. This election of one branch of the federal by the state legislatures, secures an absolute dependence of the former on the latter. The biennial exclusion of one third will lessen the facility of a combination, and may put a stop to intrigues. I appeal to our past experience, whether they will attend to the interests of their constituent states. Have not those gentlemen, who have been honored with seats in Congress, *often signalized themselves by their attachment to their seats?* I wish this government may answer the expectation of its friends, and foil the apprehension of its enemies. I hope the patriotism of the people will continue, and be a sufficient guard to their liberties. I believe its tendency will be, that the state governments will counteract the general interest, and ultimately prevail. The number of the representatives is yet sufficient for our safety, and will gradually increase; and, if we consider their different sources of information, the number will not appear too small.

GREAT
SPEECHES
IN
HISTORY

The Native
American
Speaks

You Must Lift the Hatchet Against the English

Pontiac

In this allegorical speech, the Ottawan leader Pontiac,
who led some of the largest forces against the British,
tries to inspire confidence in his plan for armed resistance. Pontiac, a staunch opponent of the British, had allied himself with the French, fighting with them at Fort
Duquesne in 1755 when General Edward Braddock was
defeated. Later, Pontiac was the leader of a group of
loosely confederated tribes and had plans for expanding
into areas that the British were increasingly claiming as
their own. By the early 1760s, he had decided that a concerted attack was needed on the British line of defense on
the western front. The plan was to attack forts and trading posts and kill all the inhabitants.

At an important council fire in April 1763, Pontiac
addressed the Ottawans and their neighboring allies, arguing for the need to ruthlessly remove the scourge of the
white man who had poisoned their continent. The form
of this speech is a metaphorical narrative—a marked contrast with the legalistic style of orations of many contemporary European Americans—and it highlights the colorful metaphors and natural imagery that are often found
in Native American speeches.

Pontiac relates the story of a vision wherein a god
advises a Native American brave to put less importance
on trade goods and to resist the influx of white settlers.
The speech, although a colorful narrative, has several

From Pontiac's speech "You Must Lift the Hatchet Against Them," delivered at
an Indian council meeting near Detroit, Michigan, April 17, 1763, as reprinted in
Indian Oratory, edited by W.C. Vanderwerth (Norman: University of Oklahoma
Press, 1971).

specific exhortations. Through the figure of the brave, Pontiac advocates a return to the precolonial weaponry of bows and arrows and a refusal to trade furs for European luxuries and trinkets. He harshly condemns the deleterious effects of European alcohol, and more generally, he urges the destruction of the English settlers and the revival of the traditional Ottawan way of life.

A Delaware Indian conceived an eager desire to learn wisdom from the Master of Life; but, being ignorant where to find him, he had recourse to fasting, dreaming, and magical incantations. By these means it was revealed to him, that, by moving forward in a straight, undeviating course, he would reach the abode of the Great Spirit. He told his purpose to no one, and having provided the equipments of a hunter—gun, powder-horn, ammunition, and a kettle for preparing his food—he set out on his errand. For some time he journeyed on in high hope and confidence. On the evening of the eighth day, he stopped by the side of a brook at the edge of a meadow, where he began to make ready his evening meal, when, looking up, he saw three large openings in the woods before him, and three well-beaten paths which entered them. He was much surprised; but his wonder increased, when, after it had grown dark, the three paths were more clearly visible than ever. Remembering the important object of his journey, he could neither rest nor sleep; and, leaving his fire, he crossed the meadow, and entered the largest of the three openings. He had advanced but a short distance into the forest, when a bright flame sprang out of the ground before him, and arrested his steps. In great amazement, he turned back, and entered the second path, where the same wonderful phenomenon again encountered him; and now, in terror and bewilderment, yet still resolved to persevere, he took the last of the three paths. On this he journeyed a whole day without interruption, when at length, emerging from the forest, he saw before him a vast mountain, of dazzling whiteness. So precipitous was the ascent that the Indian thought it hopeless to go farther, and looked around him in despair; at that moment, he saw, seated at some distance above, the figure of a beautiful woman arrayed in white, who arose as he looked upon her, and thus accosted him:

Advice

"How can you hope, encumbered as you are, to succeed in your design? Go down to the foot of the mountain, throw away your gun, your ammunition, your provisions, and your clothing; wash yourself in the stream which flows there, and you will then be prepared to stand before the Master of Life."

The Indian obeyed, and again began to ascend among the rocks, while the woman, seeing him still discouraged, laughed at his faintness of heart, and told him that, if he wished for success, he must climb by the aid of one hand and one foot only. After great toil and suffering, he at length found himself at the summit. The woman had disappeared, and he was left alone. A rich and beautiful plain lay before him, and at a little distance he saw three great villages, far superior to the squalid wigwams of the Delawares. As he approached the largest, and stood hesitating whether he should enter, a man gorgeously attired stepped forth, and, taking him by the hand, welcomed him to the celestial abode. He then conducted him into the presence of the Great Spirit, where the Indian stood confounded at the unspeakable splendor which surrounded him. The Great Spirit bade him be seated, and thus addressed him:

The Vision

"I am the Maker of heaven and earth, the trees, lakes, rivers, and all things else. I am the Maker of mankind; and because I love you, you must do my will. The land on which you live I have made for you, and not for others. Why do you suffer the white men to dwell among you? My children, you have forgotten the customs and traditions of your forefathers. Why do you not clothe yourselves in skins, as they did, and use the bows and arrows, and the stone-pointed lances, which they used? You have bought guns, knives, kettles, and blankets, from the white men, until you can no longer do without them; and, what is worse, you have drunk the poison fire-water, which turns you into fools. Fling all these things away; live as your wise forefathers lived before you. And as for these English—these dogs dressed in red, who have come to rob you of your hunting-grounds, and drive away the game—you must lift the hatchet against them. Wipe them from the face of the earth, and then you will win my favor back again, and once more be happy and prosperous. The children of your great father, the King of France, are not like the English. Never forget that they are your brethren. They are very dear to me, for they love the red men, and understand the true mode of worshipping me."

Speech to George Washington

Cornplanter

Cornplanter, chief of the Senecas, and his tribesmen had fought with the British against the American revolutionary troops during the War of Independence. Afterwards, at the signing of the Treaty of Fort Stanwix, the Senecas were among the Native American tribes forced to cede all the land west of the Niagara River to the American government. The Senecas consoled themselves, however, with the belief that over time relations with the Americans would improve, and they might regain some of their lost lands. This did not happen; instead, the pressure to sell more land only increased. In addition, the Native Americans were often robbed and attacked by whites.

In 1790, Cornplanter traveled to Philadelphia and delivered a speech to George Washington in which he recounted several years' worth of complaints: lost land, murder, robberies, swindles by shopkeepers, and a host of other grievances that the Senecas had suffered at the hands of white people. Cornplanter expressed his ongoing desire for peace and harmony with the white people, and to this end, he asked Washington to help in several practical ways. He requested financial compensation for several robberies and murders perpetrated by white people, the establishment of a shop run by someone the Senecas knew to be trustworthy, and the provision of a representative to whom the Senecas could communicate their problems. Cornplanter asked that an interpreter be appointed in order to mediate in daily affairs, for when crimes were committed against the Senecas, they not only

From Cornplanter's speech to George Washington, delivered in Philadelphia, Pennsylvania, October 29, 1790, as reprinted in *Indian Oratory*, edited by W.C. Vanderwerth (Norman: University of Oklahoma Press, 1971).

had no jurisdiction to punish the perpetrators, but they also had no representation to voice their complaints.

When addressing President Washington, Cornplanter repeatedly employed the respectful appellation of "father" instead of the more egalitarian "brother" in order to signal the superior power of the Americans. Thus instead of attempting to talk of rights or justice, he appealed to the typically Christian virtues of pity, mercy, and love in his efforts to procure justice and representation for his people.

The Fathers of the Quaker State, Obeale or Cornplanter, returns thanks to God for the pleasure he has in meeting you this day with six of his people.

Fathers: Six years ago I had the pleasure of making peace with you, and at that time a hole was dug in the earth, and all contentions between my nation and you ceased and were buried there.

Treaty of Fort Stanwix

At a treaty then held at Fort Stanwix between the six nations of Indians and the Thirteen Fires [white Americans], three friends from the Quaker State came to me and treated with me for the purchase of a large tract of land upon the northern boundary of Pennsylvania, extending from Tioga to Lake Erie for the use of their warriors. I agreed to sale of the same, and sold it to them for four thousand dollars. I begged of them to take pity on my nation and not buy it forever. They said they would purchase it forever, but that they would give me further one thousand dollars in goods when the leaves were ready to fall, and when I found that they were determined to have it, I agreed that they should have it. I then requested, as they were determined to have the land, to permit my people to have the game and hunt upon the same, which request they complied with, and promised me to have it put upon record, that I and my people should have that privilege.

Fathers: The six nations then requested that another talk

might be held with the Thirteen Fires, which was agreed to, and a talk afterwards held between them at Muskingum. Myself with three of my chiefs attended punctually, and were much fatigued in endeavoring to procure the attendance of the other nations, but none of them came to the council fire except the Delawares and the Wyandots.

Fathers: At the same treaty the Thirteen Fires asked me on which side I would die, whether on their side, or the side on those nations who did not attend the council fire. I replied, listen to me fathers of the Thirteen Fires, I hope you will consider how kind your fathers were treated by our fathers, the six nations, when they first came into this country, since which time you have become strong, insomuch, that I now call you fathers.

In former days when you were young and weak, I used to call you brother, but now I call you father. Father, I hope you will take pity on your children, for now I inform you that I'll die on your side. Now, father, I hope you will make my bed strong.

Land Sales

Fathers of the Quaker State: I speak but little now, but will speak more when the Thirteen Fires meet, I will only inform you further, that when I had finished my talk with the Thirteen Fires, General Gibson, who was sent by the Quaker State, came to the fire, and said that the Quaker State had bought of the Thirteen Fires a tract of land extending from the northern boundary of Pennsylvania at Connewango River to Buffaloe Creek on Lake Erie, and thence along the said lake to the northern boundary of Pennsylvania aforesaid. Hearing this I run to my father, and said to him, father have you sold this land to the Quaker State, and he said he did not know, it might have been done since he came there. I then disputed with Gibson and Butler, who was with him about the same, and told them I would be satisfied if the line was run from Connewango River through Chatochque Lake to Lake Erie, for Gibson and Butler had told me that the Quaker State had purchased the land from the Thirteen Fires, but that not withstanding the Quaker State had given to me one thousand dollars in fine prime goods which were ready for me and my people at Fort Pitt, we then agreed that the line should be run from Connewango River through Chatochque Lake into Lake Erie, and that one-half of the fish in Chatochque Lake should be mine and one-half theirs.

They then said as the Quaker State had purchased the whole from the Thirteen Fires, that the Thirteen Fires must pay back to the Quaker State the value of the remaining land. When I heard this my mind was at ease, and I was satisfied.

I then proposed to give a half mile square of land upon the line so agreed upon to a Mr. Hartzhorn who was an ensign in General Harmar's army out to a Mr. Britt, a cadet who acted as a clerk upon occasion, and who I well know by the name of Half-Town, for the purpose of their settling there to prevent any mischief being committed in future upon my people's lands, and I hoped that the Quaker State would in addition thereto give them another half mile square on their side of the line so agreed upon for the same purpose, expecting thereby that the line so agreed upon would be known with sufficient certainty and that no disputes would thereafter arise between my people and the Quaker State concerning it. I then went to my father of the Thirteen Fires and told him I was satisfied, and the coals being covered up I said to my children you must take your course right through the woods to Fort Pitt. When I was leaving Muskingum my own son who remained a little while behind to warm himself at the fire was robbed of a rifle by one of the white men, who, I believe, to have been a Yankee. Myself with Mr. Joseph Nicholson and a Mr. Morgan then travelled three days together through the wilderness, but the weather being very severe they were obliged to separate from me, and I sent some of my own people along with Mr. Nicholson and Mr. Morgan as guides to conduct them on to Wheelen.

The Journey

After I had separated from Mr. Nicholson and Mr. Morgan, I had under my charge one hundred and seventy persons of my own nation, consisting of men, women and children to conduct through the wilderness through heaps of briars, and having lost our way, we, with great difficulty reached Whee-len. When arrived there being out of provision I requested of a Mr. Zanes to furnish me and my people with bacon and flour to the amount of seventeen dollars, to be paid for out of goods belonging to me and my people at Fort Pitt. Having obtained my request, I proceeded on my journey for Pitts-burg, and about ten miles from Wheelen my party were fired upon by three white people, and one of my people in the rear of my party received two shot through his blanket.

Fathers: It was a constant practice with me throughout the whole journey to take great care of my people, and not suffer them to commit any outrages or drink more than their necessities required. During the whole of my journey only one accident happened which was owing to the kindness of the people of the town called Catfish, in the Quaker State, who, while I was talking with the head men of the town, gave to my people more liquor than was proper, and some of them got drunk, which obliged me to continue there with my people all night, and in the night my people were robbed of three rifles and one shot gun; and though every endeavor was used by the head men of the town upon complaint made to them to discover the perpetrators of the robbery, they could not be found; and on my people's complaining to me I told them it was their own fault by getting drunk.

Fathers: Upon my arrival at Fort Pitt I saw the goods which I had been informed of at Muskingum, and one hun-dred of the blankets were all moth eaten and good for noth-ing, I was advised not to take the blankets, but the blankets which I and my people then had being all torn by the briars in our passage through the wilderness, we were under the ne-cessity of taking them to keep ourselves warm; and what most surprised me, was that after I had received the goods they extinguished the fire and swept away the ashes, and having no interpreter there I could talk with no one upon the subject. Feeling myself much hurt upon the occasion, I wrote a letter to you Fathers of the Quaker State, complaining of the injury, but never received any answer. Having waited a considerable time, and having heard that my letter got lost, I wrote a second time to you Fathers of the Quaker State and then I received an answer.

A Representative Is Needed

I am very thankful to have received that answer, and as the answer intreated me to come and speak for myself, I thank God that I have this opportunity, I therefore speak to you as follows. I hope that you, the Fathers of the Quaker State, will fix some person at Fort Pitt to take care of me and my people. I wish, and it is the wish of my people if agreeable to you that my present interpreter, Joseph Nicholson, may be the person, as I and my people have a confidence in him, and are satisfied that he will always exert himself to preserve peace and harmony between you and us. My reasons for wishing an interpreter to be placed there, are that often times when my hunters and people come there, their canoes and other things are stolen, and they can obtain no redress, not having any person there on whom they can rely to interpret for them and see justice done to them.

Fathers of the Quaker State: About a year ago a young man, one of my tribe who lived among the Shawanese, was one of a party who had committed some outrages and stolen a quantity of skins the property of David Duncan, being at Fort Pitt, was seized by the white people there who would have put him into confinement and perhaps to death had not some of the chiefs of the Seneca Nation interfered and bound themselves to the said David Duncan, who insisted upon satisfaction, for payment of the sum of five hundred and thirty dollars for the said skins so stolen, upon which the young man aforesaid was released and delivered up to them.

Murder and Robbery

Fathers of the Quaker State: I wish now to acquaint you with what happened to one of my people about four years ago, four miles above Fort Pitt: A young man who was married to my wife's sister, when he was hunting, was murdered by a white man. There were three reasons for his being killed: In the first place he had a very fine riding horse; secondly, he was very richly dressed, and had about him a good deal of silver; and thirdly, he had with him a very fine rifle. The white man invited him to his house, to light from his horse, and as he was getting off his horse, his head being rather down, the white man struck him with a tomahawk on the head and killed him, and having plundered him dragged him into the river. Upon discovery of the murder, my people, with Mr. Nicholson and Mr. Duncan, had a great deal of trouble, and took a great deal of pains to find out the person who had committed the murder, and after three days' searching, they discovered him.

Fathers of the Quaker State: About five years ago, one of my chiefs, name Half-Town, was sent to Fort Pitt to deliver up into your hands your own flesh and blood who were taken in the war, and before he returned two horses were stolen from him by the white people. Now, Fathers, I will inform you of another accident which happened to my people last winter, fifteen miles below Fort Pitt. My nephew, with a hunting party, being there, was shot through the head in Mr. Nicholson's camp, the particulars of which Mr. Nicholson, who is here present, can inform you.

Well, Fathers, I beg of you once more not to let such bad people be 'longside of me. And, Fathers, you must not think I or any of my people are bad or wish evil to you and yours, nor must you blame us for mischiefs that have been committed by the other nations. Fathers, consider me and my people, and the many injuries we have sustained by the repeated robberies, and in the murders and depredations committed by the whites against us.

We Wish Peace

It is my wish and the wishes of my people to live peaceably and quietly with you and yours, but the losses we have sustained require some compensation. I have, with the consent of my people, agreed to receive from you eight hundred and thirty dollars, as a satisfaction for all losses and injuries I and my people have sustained, and this being paid me by you, to enable me to satisfy such of my people as have sustained those losses and suffered those injuries, we shall, I hope, in future live peaceable together, and bury in the earth all ill will and enmity to each other.

Fathers of the Quaker State: I have now had the pleasure

to meet you with six of my people. We have come a great way, by your desire, to talk with you and to show to you the many injuries my nation has sustained. It now remains with you to do with me and my people what you please, on account of the present trouble which I and my people have taken for your satisfaction, and in compliance with your request.

Fathers, having come this great way at your request, and as it is necessary for some of us to remain here to talk with the Thirteen Fires when they meet, I have concluded to send back four of my people, and to remain here myself with Half-Town and my interpreter, Mr. Nicholson, until that time, which I hope you will approve of. But should you not approve of it, I must be under the necessity of returning with the whole of my people, which will be attended with a considerable expense.

A General Store

Fathers of the Quaker State: You have now got the most of our lands, and have taken the game upon the same. We have only the privilege of hunting and fishing thereon. I, therefore, would make this further request, that a store may be established at Fort Pitt for the accommodation of my people and the other nations when they go out to hunt; and where they may purchase goods at a reasonable price. For, believe me, Fathers, you yourselves would be frightened were you to know the extravagant prices we are obliged to pay for the goods we purchase.

There is a man (Esquire Wilkie) in Pittsburg, who has taken a great deal of pains to serve my people, and has pitied them; my people, when there, are very kindly treated by him, and give him a great deal of trouble, but he thinks nothing of it; he is the man my people wish should have charge of the store.

Fathers of the Quaker State: I have heard that you have been pleased to present to me a tract of land, but as yet I have not seen no writings for the same; well, Fathers, if it is true that you have given me this tract of land, I can only thank you for the same, but I hope you will also give me tools and materials for working the same.

Reward for Nicholson

Fathers of the Quaker State: Five years ago, when I used to be with my present interpreter, Joseph Nicholson, he took care of me and my people. Considering his services and the difficulties he underwent in his journey from Muskingum to Fort Pitt, the Six Nations wished to have him seated upon a tract of land of six miles square, lying in the forks of Allegany River, and Broken Straw creek, and accordingly patented the same to him, this being the place where the battle was fought between my people and yours, and where about thirty of my people were beaten by him and twenty-five of your people, and where he was shot through the thigh. Now, Fathers, it is my wish, and I tell you it is the wish of the whole Six Nations, in behalf of whom and myself, I request that you would grant and confirm to our brother and friend, the before named Joseph Nicholson, the aforesaid tract of land, as described in our patent or grant to him.

This, Fathers, is all I have to say to the Quaker State, and I hope you will consider well all I have mentioned.

A Rejection of the White Man's Religion

Red Jacket

The occasion of this speech was the visit of a Protestant preacher from the Massachusetts Evangelical Missionary Society, who sought permission to establish a mission on Seneca land. For decades, the Spanish, French, and British had been proselytizing Native Americans, and the result, believed Red Jacket, was only a disastrous loss of traditional tribal values and religion.

In general, the American government encouraged missionary efforts, and when a church wished to establish a mission, a U.S. official would assist them in seeking consent from Native American leaders. In the summer of 1805, missionary Cram arrived with a government agent for this purpose, and a council of Seneca leaders met and lit a fire in honor of the discussions.

Cram's tone was condescending and patronizing. He told the gathered Senecas that he had come "to instruct you how to worship the Great Spirit agreeably to his mind and will." He continued by threatening misery for those who failed to conform to his beliefs, stating: "There is but one religion, and but one way to serve God, and if you do not embrace the right way you cannot be happy hereafter."

In the following speech, the Seneca chief's response to Cram, Red Jacket points out that different peoples have different ways of worshiping God, and he doubts whether Christianity was intended for the Senecas. Red Jacket expresses his satisfaction with his own religion,

From Red Jacket, "Brother, the Great Spirit Has Made Us All," delivered at an Indian council meeting near Buffalo, New York, 1805, as reprinted in *The World's Best Orations*, edited by David J. Brewer (Chicago: Ferd. P. Kaiser, 1923).

and suggests that despite the differences between the two faiths, he believes that the Senecas' religion is in no way inferior to Christianity.

Red Jacket's eloquent response so angered Cram that the missionary stormed off in a rage, rudely refusing to shake the hands of his Seneca hosts or to extinguish the fire that had been lit in his honor.

*F*riend and Brother:—
It was the will of the Great Spirit that we should meet together this day. He orders all things, and has given us a fine day for our council. He has taken his garment from before the sun, and caused it to shine with brightness upon us. Our eyes are opened, that we see clearly; our ears are unstopped, that we have been able to hear distinctly the words you have spoken. For all these favors we thank the Great Spirit; and him only.

Brother: This council fire was kindled by you. It was at your request that we came together at this time. We have listened with attention to what you have said. You requested us to speak our minds freely. This gives us great joy; for we now consider that we stand upright before you, and can speak what we think. All have heard your voice, and all speak to you now as one man. Our minds are agreed.

Brother: You say you want an answer to your talk before you leave this place. It is right you should have one, as you are a great distance from home, and we do not wish to detain you. But we will first look back a little, and tell you what our fathers have told us, and what we have heard from the white people.

A Plentiful Past

Brother: Listen to what we say. There was a time when our forefathers owned this great island. Their seats extended from the rising to the setting sun. The Great Spirit had made it for the use of Indians. He had created the buffalo, the deer, and other animals for food. He had made the bear and the beaver. Their skins served us for clothing. He had scattered them over the country, and taught us how to take them. He had caused the earth to produce corn for bread. All this he had done for his red children, because he loved them. If we had some disputes about our hunting ground, they were generally settled without the shedding of much blood. But an evil day came upon us. Your forefathers crossed the great water, and landed on this island. Their numbers were small. They found friends, and not enemies. They told us they had fled from their own country for fear of wicked men, and had come here to enjoy their religion. They asked for a small seat. We took pity on them, granted their request, and they sat down amongst us. We gave them corn and meat; they gave us poison (whisky) in return.

The white people, brother, had now found our country. Tidings were carried back, and more came amongst us. Yet we did not fear them. We took them to be friends. They called us brothers. We believed them, and gave them a larger seat. At length their numbers had greatly increased. They wanted more land; they wanted our country. Our eyes were opened, and our minds became uneasy. Wars took place. Indians were hired to fight against Indians, and many of our people were destroyed. They also brought strong liquor amongst us. It was strong and powerful, and has slain thousands.

Brother: Our seats were once large, and yours were small. You have now become a great people, and we have scarcely a place left to spread our blankets. You have got our country, but are not satisfied; you want to force your religion upon us.

Your Religion Is Not for Us

Brother: Continue to listen. You say that you are sent to instruct us how to worship the Great Spirit agreeably to his mind; and if we do not take hold of the religion which you white people teach, we shall be unhappy hereafter. You say that you are right, and we are lost. How do we know this to be true? We understand that your religion is written in a book. If it were intended for us as well as you, why has not the Great Spirit given to us, and not only to us, but why did he not give to our forefathers the knowledge of that book, with the means of understanding it rightly? We only know what you tell us about it. How shall we know when to believe, being so often deceived by the white people?

Brother: You say there is but one way to worship and serve the Great Spirit. If there is but one religion, why do you white people differ so much about it? Why not all agreed, as you can all read the book?

Red Jacket

Brother: We do not understand these things. We are told that your religion was given to your forefathers, and has been handed down from father to son. We also have a religion, which was given to our forefathers and has been handed down to us, their children. We worship in that way. It teaches us to be thankful for all the favors we receive; to love each other, and to be united. We never quarrel about religion.

Brother: The Great Spirit has made us all, but he has made a great difference between his white and red children. He has given us different complexions and different customs. To you he has given the arts. To these he has not opened our eyes. We know these things to be true. Since he has made so great a difference between us in other things, why may we not conclude that he has given us a different religion according to our understanding? The Great Spirit does right. He knows what is best for his children; we are satisfied.

Brother: We do not wish to destroy your religion, or take it from you. We only want to enjoy our own.

Brother: You say you have not come to get our land or our money, but to enlighten our minds. I will now tell you that I have been at your meetings, and saw you collect money from the meeting. I cannot tell what this money was intended for, but suppose that it was for your minister, and if we should conform to your way of thinking, perhaps you might want some from us.

Brother: We are told that you have been preaching to the white people in this place. These people are our neighbors. We are acquainted with them. We will wait a little while, and see what effect your preaching has upon them. If we find it does them good, makes them honest, and less disposed to cheat Indians, we will then consider again of what you have said.

Brother: You have now heard our answer to your talk, and this is all we have to say at present. As we are going to part, we will come and take you by the hand, and hope the Great Spirit will protect you on your journey, and return you safe to your friends.

The Land Cannot Be Sold

Tecumseh

By the early nineteenth century, white settlers had colonized the land from the eastern coast through to the Great Plains of the Midwest. Often, settlers would claim these territories on the basis that they had "bought" them from a certain chief, and a contract would be furnished to provide legitimacy for the takeover of Native American lands. Tecumseh, a prominent Shawnee leader at this time, clearly saw through this legalistic guise of authority and protested both the practice of land acquisition and the practice of getting Indians drunk in order to make it easier to buy their land. In the following address made to William Henry Harrison (then governor of Indiana and later U.S. president), he objects to the fundamental philosophy that such tactics are based on: the belief that land belongs to one person or one tribe. He attempts to explain that in Native American culture, there is no such notion as private ownership of land—ownership is communal among all the people who wish to use the land, for the earth belongs to God and not to man. Just as the concept of signing away the air or the sky seems absurd, so too the notion of one chief selling the land that belongs to many tribes is incomprehensible to Native Americans.

Houses are built for you to hold councils in; Indians hold theirs in the open air. I am a Shawnee. My forefathers were warriors. Their son is a warrior. From

From Tecumseh's speech, "Sell a Country! Why Not Sell the Air?" delivered to Gov. William Henry Harrison, Indiana, August 12, 1810, as reprinted in *I Have Spoken: American History Through the Voices of the Indians*, compiled by Virginia Irving Armstrong (Athens, OH: Swallow Press/Ohio University Press, 1971).

them I take my only existence. From my tribe I take nothing. I have made myself what I am. And I would that I could make the red people as great as the conceptions of my own mind, when I think of the Great Spirit that rules over us all. . . . I would not then come to Governor Harrison to ask him to tear up the treaty. But I would say to him, "Brother, you have the liberty to return to your own country."

You wish to prevent the Indians from doing as we wish them, to unite and let them consider their lands as the common property of the whole. You take the tribes aside and advise them not to come into this measure. . . . You want by your distinctions of Indian tribes, in allotting to each a particular, to make them war with each other. You never see an Indian endeavor to make the white people do this. You are continually driving the red people, when at last you will drive them onto the great lake, where they can neither stand nor work.

One Chief Cannot Sell the Land of Many Tribes

Since my residence at Tippecanoe, we have endeavored to level all distinctions, to destroy village chiefs, by whom all mischiefs are done. It is they who sell the land to the Americans. Brother, this land that was sold, and the goods that was given for it, was only done by a few. . . . In the future we are prepared to punish those who propose to sell land to the Americans. If you continue to purchase them, it will make war among the different tribes, and, at last I do not know what will be the consequences among the white people. Brother, I wish you would take pity on the red people and do as I have requested. If you will not give up the land and do cross the boundary of our present settlement, it will be very hard, and produce great trouble between us.

The way, the only way to stop this evil is for the red men to unite in claiming a common and equal right in the land, as it was at first, and should be now—for it was never divided, but belongs to all. No tribe has the right to sell, even to each other, much less to strangers. . . . *Sell a country! Why not sell the air, the great sea, as well as the earth?* Did not the Great

Spirit make them all for the use of his children?

How can we have confidence in the white people?

When Jesus Christ came upon the earth you killed him and nailed him to the cross. You thought he was dead, and you were mistaken. You have Shakers among you and you laugh and make light of their worship.

Everything I have told you is the truth. The Great Spirit has inspired me.

A Call to Fight

Black Hawk

The history of European and Native American relations
in the eighteenth and nineteenth centuries comprises a
string of broken treaties amidst a program of ruthless
colonialist expansion. European aspirations for controlling the western territories escalated as the population
increased, and the indigenous inhabitants of North
America were pushed further and further out of their ancestral lands and into undesirable mountainous or arid
regions. This was especially true after 1815, when the
1812 war with Britain had ended, the Napoleonic wars
were over, and a series of poor harvests prompted ag-
gressive western expansion.

The Native Americans depended on arable land and
forest or river access for their hunting, fishing, and farming, and often found themselves unable to physically sus-
tain themselves on their new terrain. Such was the situation of the Sauk people, who were starving as their
erstwhile vast territories flanking both banks of the Mississippi had been reduced to a smaller, more arid area on the
western bank that was incapable of supporting the tribe.

After several decades of increasing hardships, the
pacifist Sauk chief Keokuk continued to advocate peace,
but Black Hawk, the pugnacious former chief of the Sauk
people, decided that the only option available to the
Sauk was armed attack. In the following speech, he re-
cites a litany of charges against the white man in an effort to incite his tribesmen to war. Months later, describing this moment, Black Hawk recalled, "Things were
getting worse. . . .We called a great council and built a
fire. The spirits of our fathers arose and spoke to us to
avenge our wrongs or die."

From Black Hawk's speech, "A Rally to Fight," delivered at an Indian council
meeting, April 1832, as reprinted in *Indian Oratory*, edited by W.C. Vanderwerth
(Norman: University of Oklahoma Press, 1971).

Black Hawk, who was by then in his mid-sixties, re-calls in his oratory a glorious past in which land and food were abundant, contrasting that former plethora with the current paucity of resources. Central to Black Hawk's argument is the point that the Native Americans have repeatedly been forced to relinquish their land through coercive and immoral means. Calling for unity among his people, he reviles the use of European-imported alcohol and forced land acquisitions and makes a stirring plea for the necessity of war.

The Sauk rebellion, however, was short-lived. Black Hawk and his men crossed over to the east side of the Mississippi, but were soon met by U.S. troops. Sauk losses were heavy, and Black Hawk was captured by several Winnebago Indians on August 27, 1832, and taken prisoner at Prairie du Chien.

Head-men, Chiefs, Braves and Warriors of the Sauks: For more than a hundred winters our nation was a powerful, happy and united people. The Great Spirit gave to us a territory, seven hundred miles in length, along the Mississippi, reaching from Prairie du Chien to the mouth of the Illinois river. This vast territory was composed of some of the finest and best land for the home and use of the Indian ever found in this country. The woods and prairies teemed with buffalo, moose, elk, bear and deer, with other game suitable to our enjoyment, while its lakes, rivers, creeks and ponds were alive with the very best kinds of fish, for our food. The islands in the Mississippi were our gardens, where the Great Spirit caused berries, plums and other fruits to grow in great abundance, while the soil, when cultivated, produced corn, beans, pumpkins and squash of the finest quality and largest quantities. Our children were never known to cry of hunger, and no stranger, red or white, was permitted to enter our lodges without finding food and rest. Our nation was respected by all who came in contact with it, for we had the ability as well as the courage to defend and maintain our rights of territory, person and property against the world. Then, indeed, was it an honor to be called a Sauk, for that name was a passport to our people traveling in other territories and among other nations. But an evil day befell us when we became a divided nation, and with that division our glory deserted us, leaving us with the hearts and heels of the rabbit in place of the courage and strength of the bear.

All this was brought about by the long guns, who now claim all our territory east of the Mississippi, including Saukenuk, our ancient village, where all of us were born, raised, lived, hunted, fished and loved, and near which are our corn lands, which have yielded abundant harvests for an hundred winters, and where sleep the bones of our sacred dead, and around which cluster our fondest recollections of heroism and noble deeds of charity done by our fathers, who were Sauks, not only in name, but in courage and action. I thank the Great Spirit for making me a Sauk, and the son of a great Sauk chief, and a lineal descendant of Nanamakee, the founder of our nation.

Paleface Vipers

The Great Spirit is the friend and protector of the Sauks, and has accompanied me as your War Chief upon the war-path against our enemies, and has given me skill to direct and you the courage to achieve an hundred victories over our enemies upon the warpath. All this occurred before we became a divided nation. We then had the courage and strength of the bear, but since the division our hearts and heels are like those of the rabbit and fawn. We have neither courage nor confidence in our leaders or ourselves, and have fallen a prey to internal jealousies and petty strifes until we are no longer worthy of the illustrious name we bear. In a word, we have become subjects of ridicule and badinage,—"there goes a cowardly Sauk." All this has resulted from the white man's accursed fire-water united with our own tribal quarrels and personal jealousies. The Great Spirit created this country for the use and benefit of his red children, and placed them in full possession of it, and we were happy and contented. Why did he send the palefaces across the great ocean to take it from us? When they landed on our territory they were received as long-absent brothers whom the Great Spirit had returned to us. Food and rest were freely given them by our fathers, who treated them all the more kindly on account of their weak and helpless condition. Had our fathers the desire, they could have crushed the intruders out of existence with the same ease we kill the blood-sucking mosquitoes. Little did our fathers then think they were taking to their bosoms, and warming them to life, a lot of torpid, half-frozen and starving vipers, which in a few winters would fix their deadly fangs upon the very bosoms that had nursed and cared for them when they needed help.

From the day when the palefaces landed upon our shores, they have been robbing us of our inheritance, and slowly, but surely, driving us back, back, back towards the setting sun, burning our villages, destroying our growing crops, ravishing our wives and daughters, beating our papooses with cruel sticks, and brutally murdering our people upon the most flimsy pretenses and trivial causes.

Lost Lands

Upon our return to Saukenuk from our winter hunting grounds last spring, we found the palefaces in our lodges, and that they had torn down our fences and were plowing our corn lands and getting ready to plant their corn upon the lands which the Sauks have owned and cultivated for so many winters that our memory cannot go back to them. Nor is this all. They claim to own our lands and lodges by right of purchase from the cowardly and treacherous Quashquamme, nearly thirty winters ago, and drive us away from our lodges and fields with kicks of their cruel boots, accompanied with vile cursing and beating with sticks. When returning from an ill-fated day's hunt, wearied and hungry, with my feet stumbling with the weight of sixty-four winters, I was basely charged by two palefaces of killing their hogs, which I indignantly denied because the charges were false, but they told me I lied, and then they took my gun, powder-horn and bullet-pouch from me by violence, and beat me with a hickory stick until blood ran down my back like drops of falling rain, and my body was so lame and sore for a moon that I could not hunt or fish. They brought their accursed fire-water to our village, making wolves of our braves and warriors, and then when we protested against the sale and destroyed their bad spirits, they came with a multitude on horseback, compelling us to flee across the Mississippi for our lives, and then they burned down our ancient village and turned their horses into our growing corn.

We Must Fight

They are now running their plows through our graveyards, turning up the bones and ashes of our sacred dead, whose spirits are calling to us from the land of dreams for vengeance on the despoilers. Will the descendants of Nanamakee and our other illustrious dead stand idly by and suffer this sacrilege to be continued? Have they lost their strength and courage, and become squaws, and papooses? The Great Spirit whispers in my ear, no! Then let us be again united as a nation and at once cross the Mississippi, rekindle our watchfires upon our ancient watch-tower, and send forth the war-whoop of the again united Sauks, and our cousins, the Masquawkees, Pottawattamies, Ottawas, Chippewas, Winnebagoes and Kickapoos, will unite with us in avenging our wrongs upon the white pioneers of Illinois.

When we recross the Mississippi with a strong army, the British Father will send us not only guns, tomahawks, spears, knives and ammunition in abundance, but he will also send us British soldiers to fight our battles for us. Then will the deadly arrow and fatal tomahawk hurtle through the air at the hearts and heads of the palefaced invaders, sending their guilty spirits to the white man's place of endless punishment, and should we, while on the warpath, meet the Pauguk, our departing spirits will be led along that path which is strewn with beautiful flowers, laden with the fragrance of patriotism and heroism, which leads to the land of dreams, whence the spirits of our fathers are beckoning us on, to avenge their wrongs.

GREAT
SPEECHES
IN
HISTORY

The
Heritage
of Liberty

A Call for National Unity and Autonomy

George Washington

In 1787, George Washington was elected president of the convention that met in Philadelphia to amend the Articles of Confederation. After the ratification of the Constitution in 1789, he became the first president of the United States, swearing in on April 14, 1789. Although more experienced as a military leader than a politician, Washington handled his office with great skill and diplomacy in the first challenging years of the republic. Perhaps the largest problem was the maintenance of the newly created union, for despite Washington's nonpartisan approach, factionalism and party politics emerged with bitter clarity during these years.

It was against this background of sectionalism and partisan politics that Washington delivered his farewell speech to the nation, excerpted here. In it, Washington simply and eloquently reminded the nation of the dire importance of guarding the union against divisiveness and sounded a call for politicians to rise above party politics. Yet in reminding Americans that unity is the foundation of liberty, Washington's tone was optimistic rather than fearful, for he firmly believed in the Constitution's ability to maintain peace among the states while also preventing long-term alliances with other countries.

Washington chose his moment of farewell to articulate his firmly isolationist position which became the basis of American foreign policy for decades after. Washington sternly warned against involvement in European affairs and alliances and outlined the importance of

From George Washington, "Farewell Address," Philadelphia, Pennsylvania, September 19, 1796, as reprinted in *The World's Famous Orations*, vol. 8, edited by William Jennings Bryan (New York: Funk Wagnalls, 1906).

American neutrality and noninterference.

Extant copies of Washington's handwritten speech indicate that he passed it on to Hamilton, who modified and moderated Washington's language. Clearly the ideas are Washington's, but Hamilton's voice perhaps emerges in the fluidity of the writing.

Thе unity of government which constitutes you one people is also now dear to you. It is justly so, for it is a main pillar in the edifice of your real independence; the support of your tranquillity at home, your peace abroad; of your safety; of your prosperity; of that very liberty which you so highly prize. But as it is easy to foresee that from different causes and from different quarters much pains will be taken, many artifices employed, to weaken in your minds the conviction of this truth; as this is the point in your political fortress against which the batteries of internal and external enemies will be most constantly and actively (tho often covertly and insidiously) directed, it is of infinite moment that you should properly estimate the immense value of your national Union to your collective and individual happiness; that you should cherish a cordial, habitual, and immovable attachment to it; accustoming yourselves to think and speak of it as the palladium of your political safety and prosperity; watching for its preservation with jealous anxiety; discountenancing whatever may suggest even a suspicion that it can in any event be abandoned; and indignantly frowning upon the first dawning of every attempt to alienate any portion of our country from the rest, or to enfeeble the sacred ties which now link together the various parts.

For this you have every inducement of sympathy and of interest. Citizens, either by birth or choice, of a common country, that country has a right to concentrate your affections. The name of AMERICAN which belongs to you in your national capacity must always exalt the just pride of patriotism more than any appellation derived from local discriminations. With slight shades of difference you have the same religion, manners, habits, and political principles. You have in a common cause fought and triumphed together; the independence and liberty you possess are the work of joint counsels and joint efforts, of common dangers, sufferings, and successes.

But these considerations, however powerfully they address themselves to your sensibility, are greatly outweighed by those which apply more immediately to your interest. Here every portion of our country finds the most commanding motives for carefully guarding and preserving the union of the whole.

The North, in an unrestrained intercourse with the South, protected by the equal laws of a common government, finds in the productions of the latter great additional resources of maritime and commercial enterprise and precious materials of manufacturing industry. The South, in the same intercourse, benefiting by the agency of the North, sees its agriculture grow and its commerce expand. Turning partly into its own channels the seamen of the North, it finds its particular navigation invigorated, and while it contributes, in different ways, to nourish and increase the general mass of the national navigation, it looks forward to the protection of a maritime strength, to which itself is unequally adapted. The East, in a like intercourse with the West, already finds—and in a progressive improvement of interior communications by land and water will more and more find—a valuable vent for the commodities which it brings from abroad or manufactures at home. The West derives from the East supplies requisite to its growth and comfort, and what is perhaps of still greater consequence, it must of necessity owe the secure enjoyment of indispensable outlets for its own productions to the weight, influence, and the future maritime strength of the Atlantic side of the Union, directed by an indissoluble community of interest as one nation. Any other tenure by which the West can hold this essential advantage, whether derived from its own separate strength or from an apostate and unnatural connection with any foreign power, must be intrinsically precarious.

While, then, every part of our country thus feels an immediate and particular interest in union, all the parts combined can not fail to find in the united mass of means and efforts greater strength, greater resource, proportionably

greater security from external danger, a less frequent interruption of their peace by foreign nations; and, what is of inestimable value, they must derive from union an exemption
from those broils and wars between themselves which so
frequently afflict neighboring countries not tied together by
the same governments, which their own rivalships alone
would be sufficient to produce, but which opposite foreign
alliances, attachments, and intrigues would stimulate and
embitter. Hence, likewise, they will avoid the necessity of
those overgrown military establishments, which, under any
form of government, are inauspicious to liberty, and which
are to be regarded as particularly hostile to republican liberty. In this sense it is that your union ought to be considered as a main prop of your liberty, and that the love of the
one ought to endear to you the preservation of the other.

These considerations speak a persuasive language to
every reflecting and virtuous mind, and exhibit the continuance of the Union as a primary object of patriotic desire. Is
there a doubt whether a common government can embrace
so large a sphere? Let experience solve it. To listen to mere
speculation in such a case were criminal. We are authorized
to hope that a proper organization of the whole, with the
auxiliary agency of governments for the respective subdivi-
sions, will afford a happy issue to the experiment. It is well
worth a fair and full experiment. With such powerful and obvious motives to union affecting all parts of our country,
while experience shall not have demonstrated its impractica-
bility, there will always be reason to distrust the patriotism of
those who in any quarter may endeavor to weaken its bands.

Threats to Unity

In contemplating the causes which may disturb our Union it
occurs as a matter of serious concern that any ground should
have been furnished for characterizing parties by geographical discriminations, Northern and Southern, Atlantic and
Western; whence designing men may endeavor to excite a belief that there is a real difference of local interests and views.
One of the expedients of party to acquire influence within
particular districts is to misrepresent the opinions and aims

of other districts. You can not shield yourselves too much against the jealousies and heartburnings which spring from these misrepresentations; they tend to render alien to each other those who ought to be bound together by fraternal affection. The inhabitants of our Western country have lately had a useful lesson on this head; they have seen, in the negotiation by the executive, and in the unanimous ratification by the Senate, of the treaty with Spain [a treaty relating to the right of both nations to navigate the Mississippi River], and in the universal satisfaction at that event throughout the United States, a decisive proof how unfounded were the suspicions propagated among them of a policy in the general government and in the Atlantic States unfriendly to their interests in regard to the Mississippi; they have been witnesses to the formation of two treaties, that with Great Britain and that with Spain, which secure to them everything they could desire, in respect to our foreign relations, toward confirming their prosperity. Will it not be their wisdom to rely for the preservation of these advantages on the Union by which they were procured? Will they not henceforth be deaf to those advisers, if such there are, who would sever them from their brethren, and connect them with aliens?

Alliances and Factions

To the efficacy and permanency of your Union a government for the whole is indispensable. No alliances, however strict, between the parts can be an adequate substitute; they must inevitably experience the infractions and interruptions which all alliances in all times have experienced. Sensible of this momentous truth, you have improved upon your first essay by the adoption of a constitution of government better calculated than your former for an intimate union and for the efficacious management of your common concerns. This government, the offspring of your own choice, uninfluenced and unawed, adopted upon full investigation and mature deliberation, completely free in its principles, in the distribution of its powers, uniting security with energy, and containing within itself a provision for its own amendment, has a just claim to your confidence and your support. Respect for its authority, compliance with its laws, acquiescence in its measures, are duties enjoined by the fundamental maxims of true liberty. The basis of our political systems is the right of the people to make and to alter their constitutions of government. But the constitution which at any time exists till changed by an explicit and authentic act of the whole people is sacredly obligatory upon all. The very idea of the power and the right of the people to establish government presupposes the duty of every individual to obey the established government.

All obstructions to the execution of the laws, all combinations and associations, under whatever plausible character, with the real design to direct, control, counteract, or awe the regular deliberation and action of the constituted authorities, are destructive of this fundamental principle, and of fatal tendency. They serve to organize faction, to give it an artificial and extraordinary force; to put, in the place of the delegated will of the nation, the will of a party, often a small but artful and enterprising minority of the community: and, according to the alternate triumphs of different parties, to make the public administration the mirror of the ill-concerted and incongruous projects of fashion, rather than the organs of consistent and wholesome plans digested by common councils, and modified by mutual interests.

However combinations or associations of the above description may now and then answer popular ends, they are likely, in the course of time and things, to become potent engines, by which cunning, ambitious, and unprincipled men will be enabled to subvert the power of the people, and to usurp for themselves the reins of government, destroying afterward the very engines which have lifted them to unjust dominion.

Toward the preservation of your government and the permanency of your present happy state it is requisite not only that you steadily discountenance irregular oppositions to its acknowledged authority, but also that you resist with care the spirit of innovation upon its principles, however specious the pretexts. One method of assault may be to affect, in the forms of the Constitution, alterations which will impair the energy of the system, and thus to undermine what can not be directly overthrown. In all the changes to which you may be invited, remember that time and habit are at least as necessary to fix the true character of governments as of other human institutions; that experience is the surest standard by which to test the real tendency of the existing constitution of a country; that facility in changes, upon the credit of mere hypothesis and opinion, exposes to perpetual change, from the endless variety of hypothesis and opinion; and remember especially that for the efficient management of your common interests, in a country so extensive as ours, a government of as much vigor as is consistent with the perfect security of liberty is indispensable. Liberty itself will find in such a government, with powers properly distributed and adjusted, its surest guardian. It is, indeed, little else than a name where the government is too feeble to withstand the enterprises of faction, to confine each member of the society within the limits prescribed by the laws, and to maintain all in the secure and tranquil enjoyment of the rights of person and property.

Political Parties

I have already intimated to you the danger of parties in the State, with particular reference to the founding of them on geographical discrimination. Let me now take a more comprehensive view, and warn you in the most solemn manner against the baneful effects of the spirit of party generally.

This spirit, unfortunately, is inseparable from our nature, having its root in the strongest passions of the human mind. It exists under different shapes in all governments, more or less stifled, controlled, or repressed; but in those of the popular form it is seen in its greatest rankness, and is truly their worst enemy.

The alternate domination of one faction over another, sharpened by the spirit of revenge, natural to party dissension, which in different ages and countries has perpetrated the most horrid enormities, is itself a frightful despotism. But this leads at length to a more formal and permanent despotism. The disorders and miseries which result gradually incline the minds of men to seek security and repose in the absolute power of an individual, and sooner or later the chief of some prevailing faction, more able or more fortunate than his competitors, turns this disposition to the purposes of his own elevation, on the ruins of public liberty.

Without looking forward to an extremity of this kind (which nevertheless ought not to be entirely out of sight), the common and continued mischiefs of the spirit of party are sufficient to make it the interest and duty of a wise people to discourage and restrain it.

It serves always to distract the public councils and enfeeble the public administration. It agitates the community with ill-founded jealousies and false alarms; kindles the animosity of one part against another; foments, occasionally, riot and insurrection. It opens the doors to foreign influence and corruption, which find a facilitated access to the government itself through the channels of party passions. Thus the policy and the will of one country are subjected to the policy and will of another.

There is an opinion that parties in free countries are useful checks upon the administration of the government and serve to keep alive the spirit of liberty. This within certain limits is probably true, and in governments of a monarchical cast, patriotism may look with indulgence, if not with favor, upon the spirit of party. But in those of the popular character, in governments purely elective, it is a spirit not to be encouraged. From their natural tendency it is certain there will always be enough of that spirit for every salutary purpose. And there being constant danger of excess, the effort ought to be by force of public opinion to mitigate and assuage it. A fire not to be quenched, it demands a uniform vigilance to prevent its bursting into a flame, lest, instead of warming, it should consume. . . .

International Alliances and Quarrels

Observe good faith and justice toward all nations; cultivate peace and harmony with all. Religion and morality enjoin this conduct, and can it be that good policy does not equally enjoin it? It will be worthy of a free, enlightened, and, at no distant period, a great nation, to give to mankind the magnanimous and novel example of a people always guided by an exalted justice and benevolence. Who can doubt that, in the course of time and things, the fruits of such a plan would richly repay any temporary advantages which might be lost by a steady adherence to it? Can it be that providence has not connected the permanent felicity of a nation with its virtue? The experiment, at least, is recommended by every sentiment which ennobles human nature. Alas! is it rendered impossible by its vices?

In the execution of such a plan nothing is more essential than that permanent, inveterate antipathies against particular nations and passionate attachments for others should be excluded, and that, in place of them, just and amicable feelings toward all should be cultivated. The nation which indulges toward another an habitual hatred or an habitual fondness is in some degree a slave. It is a slave to its animosity or to its affection, either of which is sufficient to lead it astray from its duty and its interest. Antipathy in one nation against another disposes each more readily to offer insult and injury, to lay hold of slight causes of umbrage, and to be haughty and intractable, when accidental or trifling occasions of dispute occur. Hence, frequent collisions; obstinate, envenomed, and bloody contests. The nation, prompted by ill will and resentment, sometimes impels to war the government, contrary to the best calculations of policy. The government sometimes participates in the national propensity, and adopts through passion what reason would reject; at other times it makes the animosity of the nation subservient to projects of hostility instigated by pride, ambition, and other sinister and pernicious motives. The peace often, sometimes perhaps the liberty, of nations has been the victim.

So, likewise, a passionate attachment of one nation for another produces a variety of evils. Sympathy for the favorite nation, facilitating the illusion of an imaginary common interest in cases where no real common interest exists, and infusing into one the enmities of the other, betrays the former into a participation in the quarrels and wars of the latter, without adequate inducement or justification. It leads also to concessions to the favorite nation of privileges denied to others, which is apt doubly to injure the nation making the concessions by unnecessarily parting with what ought to have been retained, and by exciting jealousy, ill will, and a disposition to retaliate, in the parties from whom equal privileges are withheld. And it gives to ambitious, corrupted, or deluded citizens (who devote themselves to the favorite nation), facility to betray or sacrifice the interests of their own country without odium, sometimes even with popularity; gilding with the appearances of a virtuous sense of obligation, a commendable deference for public opinion, or a laudable zeal for public good, the base or foolish compliances of ambition, corruption, or infatuation.

As avenues to foreign influence in innumerable ways, such attachments are particularly alarming to the truly enlightened and independent patriot. How many opportunities do they afford to tamper with domestic factions, to practise the arts of seduction, to mislead public opinion, to influence or awe the public councils! Such an attachment of a small or weak toward a great and powerful nation dooms the former to be the satellite of the latter.

Against the insidious wiles of foreign influence (I conjure you to believe me, fellow citizens), the jealousy of a free people ought to be constantly awake, since history and experience prove that foreign influence is one of the most baneful foes of republican government. But that jealousy, to be useful, must be impartial, else it becomes the instrument of the very influence to be avoided, instead of a defense against it. Excessive partiality for one foreign nation and excessive dislike of another cause those whom they actuate to see danger only on one side, and serve to veil and even second the arts of influence on the other. Real patriots, who may resist the intrigues of the favorite, are liable to become suspected and odious; while its tools and dupes usurp the applause and confidence of the people, to surrender their interests.

The great rule of conduct for us, in regard to foreign nations, is, in extending our commercial relations, to have with them as little political connection as possible. So far as we have already formed engagements, let them be fulfilled with perfect good faith. Here let us stop.

Europe has a set of primary interests which to us have none, or a very remote, relation. Hence she must be engaged in frequent controversies, the causes of which are essentially foreign to our concerns. Hence, therefore, it must be unwise in us to implicate ourselves, by artificial ties, in the ordinary vicissitudes of her politics or the ordinary combinations and collisions of her friendships or enmities.

Our detached and distant situation invites and enables us to pursue a different course. If we remain one people, under an efficient government the period is not far off when we may defy material injury from external annoyance; when we may take such an attitude as will cause the neutrality we may at any time resolve upon to be scrupulously respected; when belligerent nations, under the impossibility of making acquisitions upon us, will not lightly hazard the giving us provocation; when we may choose peace or war, as our interest, guided by justice, shall counsel.

Why forego the advantages of so peculiar a situation? Why quit our own to stand upon foreign ground? Why, by interweaving our destiny with that of any part of Europe, entangle our peace and prosperity in the toils of European ambition, rivalship, interest, humor, or caprice?

Steer Clear of Permanent Alliances

It is our true policy to steer clear of permanent alliances with any portion of the foreign world—so far, I mean, as we are now at liberty to do it; for let me not be understood as capable of patronizing infidelity to existing engagements. I hold the maxim no less applicable to public than to private affairs, that honesty is always the best policy. I repeat it, therefore, let those engagements be observed in their genuine sense. But, in my opinion, it is unnecessary and would be unwise to extend them.

Taking care always to keep ourselves, by suitable establishments, on a respectable defensive posture, we may safely trust to temporary alliances for extraordinary emergencies.

Harmony, liberal intercourse with all nations, are recommended by policy, humanity, and interest. But even our commercial policy should hold an equal and impartial hand; neither seeking nor granting exclusive favors or preferences; consulting the natural course of things; diffusing and diversifying by gentle means the streams of commerce, but forcing nothing; establishing, with powers so disposed, in order to give trade a stable course, to define the rights of our merchants, and to enable the government to support them, conventional rules of intercourse, the best that present circumstances and mutual opinion will permit, but temporary, and liable to be from time to time abandoned or varied, as experience and circumstances shall dictate; constantly keeping in view that it is folly in one nation to look for disinterested favors from another; that it must pay with a portion of its independence for whatever it may accept under that character; that, by such acceptance, it may place itself in the condition of having given equivalents for nominal favors, and yet of being reproached with ingratitude for not giving more. There can be no greater error than to expect or calculate upon real favors from nation to nation. It is an illusion which experience must cure, which a just pride ought to discard.

The Principles of Democracy Will Safeguard Liberty

Thomas Jefferson

Thomas Jefferson became the third president of the United States in 1801 and gave the following oration as his inaugural speech. Succeeding President John Adams, whose term (1797–1801) had been marked by increasing party polarization, Jefferson addressed a country in which political invective had become destructive and libelous. Jefferson calls for unity between the two parties, stresses the need to rise above factionalism, and reiterates the importance of avoiding entanglements in European alliances.

Thomas Jefferson ("Mad Tom" as his enemies called him) was the leader of the Democrat-Republicans, whose name alluded to their support of democracy within the republican structure of the American model (and who later shed the Republican part of their name to become simply the Democratic Party). The Federalists (who became the Republican Party) feared that Jefferson would reproduce the radical democracy of the French Republic, along with the bloodshed and persecution of the French aristocracy.

Jefferson's political views rested on a conception of human beings as fundamentally good, moderate, and loyal, rather than evil and radical. He assumed the typical Enlightenment position that with minimal coercion and maximum education, opportunity, and positive exemplars, human character could develop in astonishing ways. He conceived of democracy as a limited govern-

From Thomas Jefferson, "Inaugural Address," March 4, 1801, as reprinted in *Orations of American Orators*, rev. ed., vol. 1 (New York: Cooperative Publication Society, 1900).

ment which granted its citizens the highest level of liberty, interfering only when one individual deprived another of fundamental rights. In his first presidential address to the nation, Jefferson calls for national unity, while outlining the principles of democracy that would ultimately supersede the elitist Hamiltonian model of government to become the foundation of the American political system.

Friends and fellow-citizens: Called upon to undertake the duties of the first executive office of our country, I avail myself of the presence of that portion of my fellow-citizens which is here assembled, to express my grateful thanks for the favor with which they have been pleased to look toward me, to declare a sincere consciousness, that the task is above my talents, and that I approach it with those anxious and awful presentiments, which the greatness of the charge, and the weakness of my powers, so justly inspire. A rising nation, spread over a wide and fruitful land, traversing all the seas with the rich productions of their industry, engaged in commerce with nations who feel power and forget right, advancing rapidly to destinies beyond the reach of mortal eye; when I contemplate these transcendent objects, and see the honor, the happiness, and the hopes of this beloved country committed to the issue and the auspices of this day, I shrink from the contemplation, and humble myself before the magnitude of the undertaking. Utterly, indeed, should I despair, did not the presence of many, whom I see here, remind me, that, in the other high authorities provided by our constitution, I shall find resources of wisdom, of virtue, and of zeal, on which to rely under all difficulties. To you, then, gentlemen, who are charged with the sovereign functions of legislation, and to those associated with you, I look with encouragement for that guidance and support which may enable us to steer with safety the vessel in which we are all embarked, amidst the conflicting elements of a troubled world.

During the contest of opinion through which we have passed, the animation of discussions and of exertions has sometimes worn an aspect which might impose on strangers unused to think freely, and to speak and to write what they think; but this being now decided by the voice of the nation, announced according to the rules of the constitution, all will of course arrange themselves under the will of the law, and unite in common efforts for the common good. All too will bear in mind this sacred principle, that though the will of the majority is in all cases to prevail, that will, to be rightful, must be reasonable; that the minority possess their equal rights, which equal laws must protect, and to violate which would be oppression. Let us then, fellow-citizens, unite with one heart and one mind, let us restore to social intercourse that harmony and affection without which liberty and even life itself are but dreary things. And let us reflect, that having banished from our land that religious intolerance under which mankind so long bled and suffered, we have yet gained little, if we countenance a political intolerance, as despotic, as wicked, and as capable of as bitter and bloody persecutions. During the throes and convulsions of the ancient world, during the agonizing spasms of infuriated man, seeking through blood and slaughter his long-lost liberty, it was not wonderful that the agitation of the billows should reach even this distant and peaceful shore; that this should be more felt and feared by some, and less by others, and should divide opinions as to measures of safety; but every difference of opinion is not a difference of principle. We have called by different names brethren of the same principle. We are all Republicans; we are all Federalists. If there be any among us who wish to dissolve this Union, or to change its republican form, let them stand undisturbed as monuments of the safety with which error of opinion may be tolerated, where reason is left free to combat it. I know, indeed, that some honest men fear that a republican government cannot be strong; that this government is not strong enough. But would the honest patriot, in the full tide of successful experiment, abandon a government which has so far kept us free and firm, on the theoretic and visionary fear, that this government, the world's best hope, may, by possibility, want energy to preserve itself? I trust not. I believe this, on the contrary, the strongest government on earth. I believe it the only one where every man, at the call of the law, would fly to the standard of the law, and would meet invasions of the public order as his own personal concern. Sometimes it is said that man cannot be trusted with the government of himself. Can he then be trusted with the government of others? Or, have we found angels in the form of kings, to govern him? Let history answer this question.

Let us then, with courage and confidence, pursue our own federal and republican principles; our attachment to union and representative government. Kindly separated by nature and a wide ocean from the exterminating havoc of one quarter of the globe; too high-minded to endure the degradation of the others, possessing a chosen country, with room enough for our descendants to the thousandth and thousandth generation, entertaining a due sense of our equal right to the use of our own faculties, to the acquisition of our own industry, to honor and confidence from our fellow-citizens, resulting not from birth, but from our actions and their sense of them, enlightened by a benign religion, professed indeed and practised in various forms, yet all of them inculcating honesty, truth, temperance, gratitude, and the love of man, acknowledging and adoring an overruling Providence, which, by all its dispensations, proves that it delights in the happiness of man here, and his greater happiness hereafter; with all these blessings, what more is necessary to make us a happy and prosperous people? Still one thing more, fellow-citizens, a wise and frugal government, which shall restrain men from injuring one another, shall leave them otherwise free to regulate their own pursuits of industry and improvement, and shall not take from the mouth of labor the bread it has earned. This is the sum of good government; and this is necessary to close the circle of our felicities.

The Principles of Democracy

About to enter, fellow-citizens, upon the exercise of duties which comprehend everything dear and valuable to you, it is proper you should understand what I deem the essential principles of our government, and consequently, those which ought to shape its administration. I will compress them within the narrowest compass they will bear, stating the general principle, but not all its limitations. Equal and exact justice to all men, of whatever state or persuasion, religious or political; peace, commerce, and honest friendship with all nations, entangling alliances with none; the support of the State governments in all their rights, as the most competent administrations for our domestic concerns, and the surest bulwarks against anti-republican tendencies; the preservation of the general government in its whole

Thomas Jefferson

constitutional vigor, as the sheet-anchor of our peace at home and safety abroad; a jealous care of the right of election by the people, a mild and safe corrective of abuses which are lopped by the sword of revolution where peaceable remedies are unprovided; absolute acquiescence in the decisions of the majority, the vital principle of republics, from which there is no appeal but to force, the vital principle and immediate parent of despotism; a well-disciplined militia, our best reliance in peace, and for the first moments of war, till regulars may relieve them; the supremacy of the civil over the military authority; economy in the public expense, that labor may be lightly burdened; the honest payment of our debts, and sacred preservation of the public faith; encouragement of agriculture, and of commerce as its handmaid; the diffusion of information, and arraignment of all abuses at the bar of the public reason; freedom of religion, freedom of the press, and freedom of person, under the protection of the *habeas corpus*, and trial by juries impartially selected. These principles form the bright constellation, which has gone before us, and guided our steps through an age of revolution and reformation. The wisdom of our sages, and blood of our heroes, have been devoted to their attainment; they should be the creed of our political faith, the text of civic instruction, the touchstone by which to try the services of those we trust; and should we wander from them in moments of error or of alarm, let us hasten to retrace our steps, and to regain the road which alone leads to peace, liberty, and safety.

I repair, then, fellow-citizens, to the post you have assigned me. With experience enough in subordinate offices to have seen the difficulties of this, the greatest of all, I have learned to expect that it will rarely fall to the lot of imperfect man, to retire from this station with the reputation and the favor which bring him into it. Without pretensions to that high confidence you reposed in our first and greatest revolutionary character, whose pre-eminent services had entitled him to the first place in his country's love, and destined for him the fairest page in the volume of faithful history, I ask so much confidence only as may give firmness and effect to the legal administration of your affairs. I shall often go wrong through defect of judgment. When right, I shall often be thought wrong by those whose positions will not command a view of the whole ground. I ask your indulgence for my own errors, which will never be intentional; and your support against the errors of others, who may condemn what they would not, if seen in all its parts. The approbation implied by your suffrage, is a great consolation to me for the past; and my future solicitude will be, to retain the good opinion of those who have bestowed it in advance, to conciliate that of others, by doing them all the good in my power, and to be instrumental to the happiness and freedom of all.

Relying then on the patronage of your good-will, I advance with obedience to the work, ready to retire from it whenever you become sensible how much better choices it is in your power to make. And may that infinite power which rules the destinies of the universe, lead our councils to what is best, and give them a favorable issue for your peace and prosperity.

American Democracy Is a Model for the World

Elias Boudinot

Historians have suggested that Elias Boudinot's July 4, 1793, oration is a direct expression of the principles of democracy that Jefferson outlined in his inaugural eight years later. Delivering this speech before the Order of the Cincinnati, Boudinot praises American liberty and argues that it is America's responsibility to show the world that the basis of good government is moral conduct and not physical force. Distinct among nations for its democratic ideals and republican system, while much of Europe was still shackled to systems of monarchy and aristocracy, America should reveal to other countries the light of liberty and justice, Boudinot argued.

Boudinot describes America's responsibilities to enlighten other nations in Christological terms. He employs the word "mission" in its religious sense, to invoke the notion that the Americans have been chosen by God to spread the word about democracy in the same way that Christian evangelists believe it their duty to share their beliefs with others. He speaks of "our political salvation," comparing the Fourth of July to commemorative religious holidays.

As the chairman of the Continental Congress of 1782–1783 and a negotiator in the Treaty of Paris, Boudinot's early career was marked by political achievements. However, this New Jersey lawyer and statesman was also an ardent proponent of evangelism. Later in his

From Elias Boudinot, "The Mission of America," delivered to the Order of the Cincinnati, Elizabethton, New Jersey, July 4, 1793, as reprinted in *The World's Best Orations*, edited by David J. Brewer (Chicago: Ferd. P. Kaiser, 1923).

life he founded the American Bible Society and worked
with Christian groups to convert various Native American tribes to Christianity. He was particularly involved
with the Cherokees, adopting a Cherokee son, editing the
Cherokee Phoenix, and propounding the importance of
establishing schools for Native American children.

G *entlemen, Brethren, and Fellow-Citizens:*—
Having devoutly paid the sacrifice of prayer and
praise to that Almighty Being, by whose favor and
mercy this day is peculiarly dedicated to the commemoration of events which fill our minds with joy and
gladness, it becomes me, in obedience to the resolutions of
our society, to aim at a further improvement of this festival,
by leading your reflections to the contemplation of those special privileges which attend the happy and important situation you now enjoy among the nations of the earth.

Is there any necessity, fellow-citizens, to spend your
time in attempting to convince you of the policy and propriety of setting apart this anniversary, for the purpose of
remembering, with gratitude, the unexampled event of our
political salvation?

Anniversaries Preserve History

The cordial testimony you have borne to this institution for
seventeen years past supersedes the necessity of an attempt of
this kind; and, indeed, if this had been the first instance of
our commemorating the day, the practice of all nations and
of all ages would have given a sanction to the measure.

The history of the world, as well sacred as profane,
bears witness to the use and importance of setting apart a
day as a memorial of great events, whether of a religious or
political nature.

No sooner had the great Creator of the heavens and the
earth finished his almighty work, and pronounced all very
good, but he set apart (not an anniversary, or one day in a
year, but) one day in seven, for the commemoration of his

inimitable power in producing all things out of nothing.

The deliverance of the children of Israel from a state of bondage to an unreasonable tyrant was perpetuated by the eating of the Paschal Lamb and enjoining it to their posterity as an annual festival forever, with a "Remember this day, in which ye came out of Egypt, out of the house of bondage.". . .

The Legacy of the American Revolution

The late revolution, my respected audience, in which we this day rejoice, is big with events that are daily unfolding themselves and pressing in thick succession, to the astonishment of a wondering world.

It has been marked with the certain characteristic of a Divine overruling hand, in that it was brought about and perfected against all human reasoning, and apparently against all human hope; and that in the very moment of time when all Europe seemed ready to be plunged into commotion and distress.

Divine Providence, throughout the government of this world, appears to have impressed many great events with the undoubted evidence of his own almighty arm. He putteth down kingdoms and he setteth up whom he pleaseth, and it has been literally verified in us that "no king prevaileth by the power of his own strength."

The first great principle established and secured by our revolution, and which since seems to be pervading all the nations of the earth, and which should be most zealously and carefully improved and gloried in by us, is the rational equality and rights of men, as men and citizens.

I do not mean to hold up the absurd idea charged upon us, by the enemies of this valuable principle, and which contains in it inevitable destruction to every government, "that all men are equal as to acquired or adventitious rights." Men must and do continually differ in their genius, knowledge, industry, integrity, and activity.

Their natural and moral characters; their virtues and vices; their abilities, natural and acquired, together with favorable opportunities for exertion, will always make men different among themselves, and of course create a pre-eminency and superiority one over another. But the equality and rights of men here contemplated are natural, essential, and unalienable, such as the security of life, liberty, and property. These should be the firm foundation of every good government, as they will apply to all nations, at all times, and may properly be called a universal law. It is apparent that every man is born with the same right to improve the talent committed to him, for the use and benefit of society, and to be respected accordingly.

We are all the workmanship of the same Divine hand. With our Creator, abstractly considered, there are neither kings nor subjects, masters nor servants, otherwise than stewards of his appointment, to serve each other according to our different opportunities and abilities, and of course accountable for the manner in which we perform our duty; he is no respecter of persons; he beholds all with an equal eye, and although "order is heaven's first law," and he has made it essential to every good government, and necessary for the welfare of every community, that there should be distinctions among members of the same society, yet this difference is originally designed for the service, benefit, and best good of the whole, and not for their oppression or destruction.

America as an Exemplar to the World

It is our duty then, as a people, acting on principles of universal application, to convince mankind of the truth and practicability of them, by carrying them into actual exercise for the happiness of our fellow-men, without suffering them to be perverted to oppression or licentiousness.

The eyes of the nations of the earth are fast opening, and the inhabitants of this globe, notwithstanding it is three thousand years since the promulgation of the precept, "Thou shalt love thy neighbor as thyself," are but just beginning to discover their brotherhood to each other, and that all men, however different with regard to nation or color, have an essential interest in each other's welfare.

Let it then be our peculiar constant care and vigilant attention to inculcate this sacred principle and to hand it down to posterity, improved by every generous and liberal practice, that while we are rejoicing in our own political and religious privileges, we may with pleasure contemplate the happy period, when all the nations of the earth shall join in the triumph of this day and one universal anthem of praise shall arise to the Universal Creator in return for the general joy.

Another essential ingredient in the happiness we enjoy as a nation, and which arises from the principles of the revolution, is the right that every people have to govern themselves in such manner, as they judge best calculated for the common benefit.

It is a principle interwoven with our Constitution, and not one of the least blessings purchased by that glorious struggle, to the commemoration of which this day is specially devoted, that every man has a natural right to be governed by laws of his own making, either in person or by his representative, and that no authority ought justly to be exercised over him, that is not derived from the people, of whom he is one.

This, fellow-citizens, is a most important practical principle, first carried into complete execution by the United States of America.

I tremble for the event, while I glory in the subject.

To you, ye citizens of America, do the inhabitants of the earth look with eager attention for the success of a measure on which their happiness and prosperity so manifestly depend.

To use the words of a famous foreigner: "You are become the hope of human nature, and ought to become its great example. The asylum opened in your land for the oppressed of all nations must console the earth."

On your virtue, patriotism, integrity, and submission to the laws of your own making, and the government of your own choice, do the hopes of men rest with prayers and supplications for a happy issue.

Be Good Citizens

Be not, therefore, careless, indolent, or inattentive, in the exercise of any right of citizenship. Let no duty, however small, or seemingly of little importance, be neglected by you.

Ever keep in mind that it is parts that form the whole, and fractions constitute the unit. Good government generally begins in the family, and if the moral character of a people once degenerates, their political character must soon follow.

A friendly consideration of our fellow-citizens, who by our free choice become the public servants and manage the affairs of our common country, is but a reasonable return for their diligence and care in our service.

The most enlightened and zealous of our public servants can do little without the exertions of private citizens to perfect what they do but form, as it were, in embryo. The highest officers of our government are but the first servants of the people and always in their power; they have, therefore, a just claim to a fair and candid experiment of the plans they form and the laws they enact for the public weal. Too much should not be expected from them; they are but men and of like passions and of like infirmities with ourselves; they are liable to err, though exercising the purest motives and best abilities required for the purpose.

Times and circumstances may change and accidents intervene to disappoint the wisest measures. Mistaken and wicked men (who cannot live but in troubled waters) are often laboring with indefatigable zeal, which sometimes proves but too successful, to sour our minds and derange the best-formed systems. Plausible pretensions and censorious insinuations are always at hand to transfer the deadly poison of jealousy, by which the best citizens may for a time be deceived.

These considerations should lead to an attentive solicitude to keep the pure unadulterated principles of our Constitution always in view; to be religiously careful in our choice of public officers; and as they are again in our power at very short periods, lend not too easily a patient ear to every invidious insinuation or improbable story, but prudently mark the effects of their public measures and judge of the tree by its fruits. . . .

Do you, my worthy fellow-citizens, of every description, wish for more lasting matter of pleasure and satisfaction in contemplating the great events brought to your minds this day? Extend, then, your views to a distant period of future time. Look forward a few years, and behold our extended forests (now a pathless wilderness) converted into fruitful fields and busy towns. Take into view the pleasing shores of our immense lakes, united to the Atlantic States by a thousand winding canals, and beautified with rising cities, crowned with innumerable peaceful fleets transporting the rich produce from one coast to another.

Add to all this, what must most please every humane and benevolent mind, the ample provision thus made by the God of all flesh, for the reception of the nations of the earth, flying from the tyranny and oppression of the despots of the Old World, and say, if the prophecies of ancient times are not hastening to a fulfillment, when this wilderness shall blossom as a rose, the heathen be given to the Great Redeemer as his inheritance, and these uttermost parts of the earth for his possession.

Who knows but the country for which we have fought and bled may hereafter become a theatre of greater events than yet have been known to mankind?

May these invigorating prospects lead us to the exercise of every virtue, religious, moral, and political. May we be roused to a circumspect conduct,—to an exact obedience to the laws of our own making,—to the preservation of the spirit and principles of our truly invaluable Constitution,— to respect and attention to magistrates of our own choice; and finally, by our example as well as precept, add to the real happiness of our fellow-men and the particular glory of our common country.

And may these great principles in the end become instrumental in bringing about that happy state of the world, when, from every human breast, joined by the grand chorus of the skies, shall arise with the profoundest reverence, that divinely celestial anthem of universal praise,—"Glory to God in the highest; peace on earth; good will towards men."

Liberty Enlightening the World

Chauncey Depew

More than one hundred years after the American Revolution, France presented the United States with the Statue of Liberty, which was to be placed near New York harbor, the portal of the New World. Chauncey Depew, a New York attorney and congressman and president of the New York Central Railroad, was given the honor of dedicating this important public monument in 1886. Although more of a businessman than a politician, Depew became quite popular for his oratory, and in this speech, he addresses the ideal of liberty that was so central to the founding of America and that continues to be integral to the conception of the country. Recalling France's military aid to the colonists during the War of Independence, and remembering the Enlightenment tradition of the French philosophers that so influenced Benjamin Franklin, Thomas Jefferson, and other advocates for independence, Depew threads a common tradition of liberty through the histories of France and America.

The French and American Revolutions occurred within fifteen years of one another and were inspired by similar ideals of liberty and democracy, along with anti-elitist and antimonarchical impulses that created post-revolutionary republics. Depew argues that these two countries were the inspiration behind the subsequent political revolutions that occurred throughout Europe during the nineteenth century. While praising the eternal power of visual images, he opines that the Statue of Liberty will come to represent both a "beacon light" to

From Chauncey Depew, speech at the dedication of the Statue of Liberty, New York, New York, October 28, 1886, as reprinted in *The World's Best Orations*, edited by David J. Brewer (Chicago: Ferd. P. Kaiser, 1923).

other nations and a torch of hope for immigrants to America. Depew's words were prophetic, for as poverty and persecution increased throughout Europe during the late nineteenth and early twentieth centuries, millions of people who sought liberty and opportunity on American shores would indeed come to identify the Statue of Liberty as the ultimate icon of America.

American liberty has been for a century a beacon light for the nations. Under its teachings and by the force of its example, the Italians have expelled their petty and arbitrary princelings and united under a parliamentary government; the gloomy despotism of Spain has been dispelled by the representatives of the people and a free press; the great German race has demonstrated its power for empire and its ability to govern itself. The Austrian monarch, who, when a hundred years ago Washington pleaded with him across the seas for the release of Lafayette from the dungeon of Olmutz, replied that "he had not the power," because the safety of his throne and his pledges to his royal brethren of Europe compelled him to keep confined the one man who represented the enfranchisement of the people of every race and country, is to-day, in the person of his successor, rejoicing with his subjects in the limitations of a Constitution which guarantees liberties, and a Congress which protects and enlarges them. Magna Charta, won at Runnymede for Englishmen, and developing into the principles of the Declaration of Independence with their descendants, has returned to the mother country to bear fruit in an open Parliament, a free press, the loss of royal prerogative, and the passage of power from the classes to the masses.

The sentiment is sublime which moves the people of France and America, the blood of whose fathers, commingling upon the battlefields of the Revolution, made possible this magnificent march of liberty and their own Republics, to commemorate the results of the past and typify the hopes of the future in this noble work of art. The descendants of Lafayette, Rochambeau, and De Grasse, who fought for us in our first struggle, and Laboulaye, Henri Martin, De Lesseps, and other grand and brilliant men, whose eloquent voices and powerful sympathies were with us in our last, conceived the idea, and it has received majestic form and expression through the genius of [Frederic] Bartholdi [architect of the Statue of Liberty].

Art Is Eternal

In all ages the achievements of man and his aspirations have been represented in symbols. Races have disappeared and no record remains of their rise or fall, but by their monuments we know their history. The huge monoliths of the Assyrians and the obelisks of the Egyptians tell their stories of forgotten civilizations, but the sole purpose of their erection was to glorify rulers and preserve the boasts of conquerors. They teach sad lessons of the vanity of ambition, the cruelty of arbitrary power, and the miseries of mankind. The Olympian Jupiter enthroned in the Parthenon expressed in ivory and gold the awful majesty of the Greek idea of the king of the gods; the bronze statue of Minerva on the Acropolis offered the protection of the patron goddess of Athens to the mariners who steered their ships by her helmet and spear; and in the Colossus of Rhodes, famed as one of the wonders of the world, the Lord of the Sun welcomed the commerce of the East to the city of his worship. But they were all dwarfs in size and pigmies in spirit beside this mighty structure and its inspiring thought. Higher than the monument in Trafalgar Square, which commemorates the victories of Nelson on the sea; higher than the Column Vendome, which perpetuates the triumphs of Napoleon on the land; higher than the towers of the Brooklyn bridge, which exhibit the latest and grandest results of science, invention, and industrial progress, this Statue of Liberty rises toward the heavens to illustrate an idea which nerved the three hundred at Thermopylae and armed the ten thousand at Marathon; which drove Tarquin from Rome and aimed the arrow of Tell; which charged with Cromwell and his Ironsides and accompanied Sidney to the block; which fired the farmer's gun at Lexington and razed the Bastille in Paris; which inspired the charter in the cabin of the Mayflower and the Declaration of Independence from the Continental Congress.

It means that with the abolition of privileges to the few and the enfranchisement of the individual; with the equality of all men before the law and universal suffrage; with the ballot secure from fraud and the voter from intimidation; with the press free and education furnished by the State for all; with liberty of worship and free speech; with the right to rise and equal opportunity for honor and fortune, the problems of labor and capital, of social regeneration and moral growth, of property and poverty, will work themselves out under the benign influences of enlightened law-making and law-abiding liberty, without the aid of kings and armies, or of anarchists and bombs.

The Light of Liberty

Through the Obelisk, so strangely recalling to us of yesterday the past of twenty centuries, a forgotten monarch says, "I am the Great King, the Conqueror, the Chastiser of Nations," and except as a monument of antiquity it conveys no meaning and touches no chord of human sympathy. But, for unnumbered centuries to come, as Liberty levels up the people to higher standards and a broader life, this statue will grow in the admiration and affections of mankind. When [Benjamin] Franklin drew the lightning from the clouds, he little dreamed that in the evolution of science his discovery would illuminate the torch of Liberty for France and America. The rays from this beacon, lighting this gateway to the continent, will welcome the poor and the persecuted with the hope and promise of homes and citizenship. It will teach them that there is room and brotherhood for all who will support our institutions and aid in our development, but that those who come to disturb our peace and dethrone our laws are aliens and enemies forever. I devoutly believe that from the unseen and the unknown two great souls have come to participate in this celebration. The faith in which they died fulfilled, the cause for which they battled triumphant, the people they loved in the full enjoyment of the rights for which they labored and fought and suffered, the spirit voices of Washington and Lafayette join in the glad acclaim of France and the United States to Liberty Enlightening the World.

Appendix of Biographies

Samuel Adams

Samuel Adams has often been called "the Father of the American Revolution," and he is important not only as an orator but also as a political visionary and a grassroots organizer. Adams was a Boston native, born there in 1722 and dying there in 1803. He attended Harvard and graduated in 1743 with plans of entering the clergy (according to his parents' wishes) but he changed course and entered politics instead. At the time of the Stamp Act (1765), he became known as a popular leader, organizing citizens into political action groups.

In 1766 he was elected to the state legislature and became a key political figure in Boston politics. After the imposition of duties on imported goods in the 1760s, Adams was instrumental in promoting the Non-Importation Association to boycott British goods. An astute propagandist, he helped found the Sons of Liberty in 1766, which were patriotic organizations that fought for independence from the British. He also helped organize the Committees of Correspondence, organizations that attempted to promote communication and unity among the colonies.

Throughout the 1760s and 1770s, Adams was what the Americans called an "active patriot" and what the British referred to as a "revolutionary agitator." He held town meetings and organized the people of Boston on numerous occasions. For example, after the Boston Massacre of March 5, 1770, Adams organized an annual commemoration with a keynote speaker. In this way, the annual memorial became an important political event that renewed animosity against the British and recharged American patriotic enthusiasm. Adams has also been held largely responsible for instigating the Boston Tea Party of 1773, and it was in recognition of his rebellious activity that General Thomas Gage specifically precluded Samuel Adams and John Hancock from the pardon he offered to all who would lay down their arms.

After many years of resistance to the British, Adams was a prominent figure in the political conventions that both preceded and followed independence. He was a delegate to the First Continental Congress in 1774 and was a key figure at the Second Continental Congress. He signed the Declaration of Independence in 1776, and he was a member of the Massachusetts Convention that ratified the Constitution in 1788. In 1789 he became the lieutenant governor of Massachusetts, and in 1794, after Hancock died, he succeeded him as governor.

Black Hawk

Born in 1767 in current-day Illinois, Black Hawk was a member of the Sauk tribe, and like his father before him, he became the chief of the Sauk in 1788. At the age of fifteen Black Hawk had already distinguished himself as an intrepid warrior, and by seventeen he had been acknowledged as a military leader and was leading war raids. In addition to his military achievements, Black Hawk was a powerful orator who tirelessly worked to resist western expansion and was often able to incite his tribesmen to war on the basis of his compelling speeches.

Black Hawk allied himself with the British (against the Americans) in an effort to ward off increasing territorial expansion into Native American lands and fought alongside the British during the 1812 war. But after a concord was reached between Britain and the United States, he abandoned hopes that any European alliances would help defend Native American rights, and he renewed the efforts to unify the tribes of the Mississippi area into a western confederation that had begun in the 1790s.

After his unsuccessful attempts to reclaim the Sauk lands east of the Mississippi, Black Hawk was captured in 1832, and was taken to President Andrew Jackson. Black Hawk met Jackson with the following words, which now seem amusingly antiquated: "I am a man and you are another."[1] Jackson sent the Sauk chief on a tour of the great cities of the eastern seaboard in an effort to convince him of the extent of white power and resources. Black Hawk was finally convinced of the impossibility and futility of resisting the white man and returned to his home on the Des Moines River, where he died in 1838.

Jonathon Boucher

Jonathon Boucher was born in England in 1738 and moved to Virginia in 1759, where he tutored and later became an Anglican minister. He preached at several churches in Virginia before settling at Queen Anne's Parish in Maryland. A staunch Loyalist (loyal to the English Crown), Boucher became thoroughly unpopular for his political views, which made their way into most of his religious sermons. He was so disliked that he claimed that he had to preach with a gun by his side. Finally, in 1775, he returned to England, where he published the sermons he had given in North America between 1763 and 1775 in a volume entitled *A View of the Causes and Consequences of the Revolution.* "On Civil Liberty" comprised the last sermon of the thirteen that he published.

Elias Boudinot

Born in Philadelphia in 1740, Elias Boudinot was of French Huguenot extraction. He received a classical education, and like many other political leaders, he was a lawyer. He entered the practice of Richard Stockton, who was a well-known New Jersey attorney, and he later married Stockton's sister.

Boudinot was active in the pre-Revolutionary political activities of the 1760s and 1770s, and in 1777 the Continental Congress appointed him commissary general of prisons. Later that year he was elected to the Continental Congress as the New Jersey delegate, and he became the head of Congress in November 1782. It was in this position of leadership that Boudinot signed the peace treaty with England that concluded the American Revolution in 1783.

In the early 1780s he resumed the practice of law, but he then returned to Congress in 1789 after the new Constitution had been ratified. In 1796 he left Congress to accept an appointment as director of the U.S. Mint during George Washington's presidency, and he remained in this position for nine years before retiring to his estate in New Jersey.

During his retirement, Boudinot engaged in scholarly and literary pursuits. He was also extremely religious, and in 1810 he became the first president of the American Bible Society, a neophyte organization to which he made large financial contributions. He was a devout believer in Christian missionary work, promoting the conversion and education of Native Americans. Toward the end of his life, in 1816, he became absorbed in his work with the Cherokee and other Native American tribes and wrote a book in which he tried to prove that Native Americans were one of the lost tribes of Israelites.

Edmund Burke

Edmund Burke, born in 1729, was one of the most famous British political philosophers and orators of the eighteenth century. His father was a solicitor, and Burke initially planned to follow in his father's footsteps; however, upon completing his studies at Trinity College in 1747, he decided that he would prefer a career studying and writing English literature. Unimpressed by his son's abandonment of the legal profession, Burke's father cut him off financially; Burke left Dublin for London and supported himself by writing for various journals.

His second work, *The Sublime and the Beautiful*, was a major contribution to the field of aesthetics and secured for Burke admission to the important literary clubs of the day and a place in the circle of the London "men of letters," as the eighteenth-century intelligentsia described themselves. Soon after, in the early 1760s, he entered politics as secretary to Lord Charles Watson-Wentworth, marquis of Rockingham, and subsequently became a member of Parliament for many years. From early on, Burke positioned himself as an ardent supporter of American liberty, favoring the American petition produced by the Stamp Act Congress. He continued to support conciliatory and nonaggressionist policies in North America, even though he was often in the minority. Burke was known for his eloquent if lengthy speeches (*Conciliation with the Colonies* is seventy pages long and took more than six hours to deliver)—contemporaries called him "the dinner-gong."

Scholars studying Burke have found, however, a curious paradox in his writings: He ardently supported American freedom, yet his response to the French Revolution was bitter and scathing. Toward the end of his life, Burke published *Reflections on the Revolution in France*, in which he strongly condemned the actions and the violence of the French Revolution. Burke's supporters saw this conservative stance as contradicting all of his former beliefs, and many of his friends, incredulous, abandoned him. Though still somewhat mystifying, contemporary historians explain this apparent contradiction by arguing that it was the enormous differences between the circumstances of the French and American Revolutions that enabled Burke to wholeheartedly support the latter while castigating the excesses of the former.

Cornplanter

Born in 1740, Cornplanter was a chief of the Seneca, one of the tribes of the Iroquois Confederacy. (The Iroquois Confederation was a group of six Native American tribes in the area of New York State and southern Ontario that consisted of the Seneca, Onondaga, Oneida, Cayuga, Tuscarora, and Mohawk.) Cornplanter was known as an important warrior, having fought with the French in the war of 1754 to 1763. Later, however, he allied himself with England and fought alongside the British during the American Revolution. In fact, in the spring of 1780 he led a raid on the Schohairie Valley, where he captured his father and other Americans. (Cornplanter's mother was a Seneca, and his father was an Irishman by the name of O'Beale.) Cornplanter assured his father that he would have either safe passage back to his wife and family or, if he wished to come and live with the Seneca people, he would set him up in a lodge with a supply of venison.

After the American Revolution, Cornplanter continued as the chief and representative of the Seneca. He frequently traveled to Philadelphia and later to Washington, D.C., in order to bring his tribe's issues to the attention of the U.S. government. He signed the 1784 Treaty of Fort Stanwix, and in return the Seneca were granted land on the Allegheny River. After a visit to England, he become greatly enamored of British culture and advocated the adoption of European farming methods in America, believing that the Native American people would do well to learn from the whites in certain matters.

Cornplanter died in 1836, when he was in his late nineties.

Chauncey Depew

Born in 1834 in Peekskill, New York, Chauncey Depew attended Yale University and graduated in 1856. He studied law, was elected to the New York Assembly at the age of twenty-seven, and within a couple of years became New York's secretary of state. In 1869 he accepted the position as legal counsel for the New York Central Railroad, working there for many years and becoming president of the railroad in 1885. In 1898 he was elected to the U.S. Senate.

Depew was a naturally eloquent speaker whose fluid style and picturesque language made him a popular after-dinner speaker in his younger days and helped build a solid reputation as an orator throughout his life. He was often asked to speak at important ceremonies, such as the opening of the Columbian World Fair in Chicago in 1892, which was a landmark occasion for American commerce and culture.

Frederick Douglass

Frederick Douglass was born on a plantation in Talbot County, Virginia, in 1817 to a black mother and a white father. He spent most of his youth as a house slave in Baltimore, Maryland, where he learned to read and write before being sent back to work at the plantation. In 1838 he managed to escape his master and flee north. He first went to New York, and then he continued north to Massachusetts, the home of the famous abolitionist William Lloyd Garrison and his American Anti-Slavery Society.

Settling in New Bedford, Massachusetts, Douglass worked as an unskilled laborer until 1841, when he was asked to speak at an anti-slavery conference in Nantucket about his experiences as a slave. His compelling command of the English language and his forceful presence so impressed his hosts that the Massachusetts Anti-Slavery Society hired him as a lecturer. Douglass was an excellent orator; in fact, certain people found it difficult to reconcile his articulate presence with his past as a slave. To dispel doubts about the veracity of his life, he published his autobiography in 1845, entitled *Narrative of the Life of Frederick Douglass, an American Slave.*

After publication, Douglass was in danger of being forcibly returned to Baltimore. Therefore, he departed for England for a two-year lecture tour; meanwhile, his friends succeeded in procuring his independence. Returning to the United States in 1847, he established a newspaper in Rochester, New York, the *North Star,* which promoted the abolition of slavery, public education, and women's rights. As an adviser to Abraham Lincoln during the Civil War, Douglass urged the president to emancipate slaves, and he campaigned to allow African American men to fight in the U.S. Army. After the war, he worked as a U.S. marshal and as recorder of deeds in Washington, D.C., and he served as the U.S. ambassador to Haiti.

Benjamin Franklin

Benjamin Franklin embodied the ultimate Enlightenment figure: a scientist who argued that nature was knowable through observation and study, a businessman who believed that success was possible through hard work and astute organization, and a statesman who held that peace and prosperity depended on straightforward communication and compromise.

Born in Boston in 1706, Franklin was the youngest of seventeen children. Although his brothers were apprenticed in various trades, the young Benjamin was taught how to read and was schooled until the age of ten, when he was pulled out of school for financial reasons. He apprenticed in his father's soap factory for several months until his threats of running away wisely persuaded his father to relocate Benjamin to his older brother James's printing shop. Here, Benjamin flourished, and he soon began writing controversial political commentaries under the alias of "Silence Dogood," which so inflamed the local authorities that James Franklin was jailed for libel. After quarreling with James, the precocious seventeen-year-old left the print shop to seek employment at another press, only to find no work available at the Boston presses. Ambitious and determined, Franklin ran away to New York; but still finding no jobs, he continued on to Philadelphia, where he arrived penniless and dirty in 1723.

In the thriving city of Philadelphia Franklin immediately secured work, and within seven years he was running his own press. By the age of twenty-seven he was known throughout the colonies for his *Poor Richard's Almanack*, which was a pithy collection of snappy aphorisms and humorous anecdotes. At forty-two, after many years in the printing business, Franklin had made enough money to retire, and he then began his career as a scientist and a diplomat. His scientific inventions ranged from an early form of flippers and a new stove to his revolutionary investigations of electricity that culminated in his discovery of the conducting power of lightning. He famously proved his hypothesis during a lightning storm in which his assistant flew a kite and, once wet, the string conducted lightning down to the metal key at the base of the kite. Fortunately Franklin survived this dangerous experiment, which killed a Swedish scientist a year later; Franklin's invention resulted in the installation of metal lightning conductors on buildings throughout the world.

Franklin also founded a society called the Junto that was responsible for the first lending library in the United States, a firefighting society, street paving, street lighting, and a city hospital. In 1751 Franklin formally entered the political arena as a delegate to the Pennsylvania Assembly, and two years later he was made postmaster for the colonies. In both of these positions Franklin consistently worked for improved communication and unity among the colonies. Although a moderate, in the 1760s and 1770s Franklin quickly came to support independence once Britain's behavior became unacceptable.

Franklin was a pivotal figure at the early Continental Congresses at the outset of the American Revolution as well as at the peace talks with Britain in 1783 that ended the war. Known as a seasoned diplomat, he was dispatched to Britain and France on several occasions: He argued against the imposition of the Stamp Tax before British Parliament in 1766, and twelve years later he was successful in persuading the French to aid the American military effort against Britain. He was present at the Congress in which Thomas Jefferson wrote the Declaration of Independence, and he was responsible for changing Jefferson's original wording—which held truths to be "sacred and undeniable"—to the less religious and more scientific verbiage of "self-evident." In his eighties, Franklin faithfully attended the Continental Congress in Philadelphia.

Franklin in many ways embodied what came to be known as "the American Dream," rising from poverty to wealth, educating himself, and fashioning himself into a multitalented person who came to be loved and admired throughout America.

Alexander Hamilton

Alexander Hamilton was born on the Caribbean island of Nevis in 1757. His mother died when he was young, and because there were doubts about the identity of his real father, Hamilton was taken in by relatives. He spent his early teenage years working at a merchant's counting house, where he appeared to have fully mastered the precepts of commerce and economics by the age of fifteen. Extant letters that he wrote as a teenager demonstrate his commercial perspicuity and social maturity. In fact, his early experience in trade and shipping shaped his interests, and although he later studied law, his practice focused on commercial and financial cases.

Hamilton was also placed under the tutelage of a Princeton graduate, and in his spare time the young Hamilton became an avid reader. After a hurricane swept the region in 1772, Hamilton wrote a moving commentary on the disaster that was published in the local newspapers, bringing his keen insight and intellectual promise to the attention of the area's elders. They decided to send Hamilton to high school in New York, and after graduation he attended Kings College (what later became Columbia University) to further his studies. At age twenty, Hamilton joined the troops fighting Britain, and he was soon made an artillery captain. Early on he distinguished himself in the New Jersey battles and joined George Washington's staff as a lieutenant colonel, becoming one of Washington's closest aides. Fluent in English and French, confident and talented, Hamilton is often described as a person of great charm and engaging character.

At the close of the war, with America in a state of political youth and economic instability, Hamilton realized the need for a strong, coordinated political and economic government. He was present at the Constitutional Convention in Philadelphia, where he argued the Federalist case with James Madison and others. In the subsequent months, as the states debated ratification, Hamilton cowrote *The Federalist Papers* with Madison and John Jay in an effort to swing public favor toward the Federalist case in New York. Yet although he resided in New York, historians tend to trace Hamilton's championing of the Federalist cause to his foreign birth, which precluded him from developing any blinding allegiance to any particular state and its local interests.

Appointed head of the treasury in 1789, Hamilton believed strongly that economic prosperity depended on solid national credit and the efficient organization of trade and economic interests. Hamilton's papers on financial issues, *The Report on Public Credit*, *National Bank*, and *The Report on Manufactures*, together outline a cohesive system for the burgeoning American economy.

In 1804 Hamilton was tragically killed in a duel with Aaron Burr.

Andrew Hamilton

Born in England in 1676, Andrew Hamilton immigrated to Virginia at the age of twenty-four and later Hamilton served as the attorney general of Pennsylvania and was the speaker for most of the twelve years that he sat in the Pennsylvania Assembly (1727–1739). During the eighteenth century, Hamilton was known as a most distinguished attorney, and he is remembered primarily for his successful defense of the New York printer accused of libel, John Peter Zenger.

John Hancock

Born in Quincy, Massachusetts, in 1737, John Hancock is remembered as the first man to sign the Declaration of Independence. Not only was he a fine businessman and reputedly the wealthiest merchant in Boston, but he was also a devoted politician with a long record of public service. After his early participation in the Stamp Act protests, he was elected to the Massachusetts legislature in 1769 and headed the Boston Town Committee the following year. He was elected president of the Massachusetts Provincial Congress in 1774, and president of the seminal Continental Congress in 1775. After independence had been won, he continued in various positions of political leadership, serving as governor of Massachusetts and chairing the Massachusetts convention that ratified the federal Constitution in 1788.

As an important figure in the political and economic realm, Hancock became a target for British animosity from early on, and customs officers were especially fond of searching his vessels. During a typical search in 1768, one of his ships, *Liberty*, which was carrying wines from Madeira, was seized by customs officials for the nonpayment of taxes. An infuriated mob attacked the British bureaucrats, who fled in terror for the nearest British stronghold and called for troops. This event was, in fact, an important factor contributing to the importation of British troops into Boston in 1768—the same troops that were later implicated in the deaths of the five Bostonians in the Boston Massacre of 1770.

Patrick Henry

Patrick Henry was born in the small town of Studley in rural western Virginia in 1736. After several failed business ventures and unsuccessful attempts at farming, he taught himself law, was admitted to the bar in 1760, and became a popular country lawyer. He soon developed a natural, enthusiastic, straightforward style of public address that won him much legal success and earned him a reputation as a forthright and gifted speaker.

Henry was elected to the Virginia General Assembly in 1765, just in time to distinguish himself during the early crisis of the Stamp Act. While other members of the assembly were complaining and discussing how to resist the measure, the young Henry surprised many by stating simply that the Stamp Act was unconstitutional and directly impinged on the liberties of the colonists. His vocal criticism of the act spread throughout the colonies through the Virginia Resolves, the resolutions that he wrote denouncing the Stamp Act.

Henry's landmark speech made in the Virginia Assembly in the wake of the Stamp Act has been lost, save for the famous anecdotal fragment wherein he exclaimed: "Caesar had his [assassin] Brutus, Charles the First his Cromwell, and George the Third . . ." The speaker of the House interrupted him with cries of "Treason! Treason!" which was echoed from other parts of the House in chorus. Apparently Henry was quite unruffled, and he continued "may profit by their example. If this be treason, make the most of it!"[2]

From the Virginia House of Burgesses, the staunch patriot was sent as the state delegate to the First Continental Congress in 1774 and later to the Second Continental Congress. Henry was elected governor of the new Commonwealth of Virginia in 1776 (a position he held until 1779) and then again from 1784 to 1786. Patrick Henry is also famous for opposing Virginia's ratification of the federal Constitution, arguing that it gave the central government too much power over the states and contained no bill of rights. He lost this battle, and he was a member of the Virginia Convention that finally decided in favor of ratifying the Constitution. He sat in the legislature from 1786 to 1790, and then he returned to the practice of law before retiring in 1794. In 1795 George Washington offered Henry the position of secretary of state, but he declined.

Thomas Jefferson

Thomas Jefferson was born in Virginia in 1743. He graduated from William and Mary College, where he studied law, and was admitted to the bar in 1767. Like George Washington, Jefferson was a native Virginian and served in the House of Burgesses from 1769 to 1775 before attending the two Continental Congresses. Jefferson then replaced Patrick Henry as the governor of Virginia (1779–1781), before succeeding Benjamin Franklin as ambassador to

France (1784–1789). Jefferson's five years in France greatly influenced him, steeping him in Enlightenment ideas of democracy and equality, human progress through knowledge, freedom through social organization, and science as a new form of truth. He was also an avid student of architecture, and after studying eighteenth-century French neoclassicism, he recreated the French style in his Virginian home, Monticello. Monticello embodied not only classical aesthetics but also notions of efficiency through good design (he had various devices built to save time and space) and the idea that architecture can shape society by organizing it in efficient ways.

Before becoming president in 1801, Jefferson served as secretary of state to Washington (1790–1794) and vice president under John Adams (1797–1801). Jefferson was president until 1809 and played an enormous role in shaping America's political institutions. Jefferson was an ardent supporter of democracy, opposing Alexander Hamilton's plan for a national bank because he thought it came dangerously close to a monarchical concentration of power. Yet despite his profound reflections on liberty and democracy, Jefferson kept hundreds of slaves at Monticello—a fact that seems strikingly contradictory from a contemporary perspective.

Jefferson is more famous as a writer than as an orator, especially for his penning of the Declaration of Independence of 1776. Jefferson himself seems to have favored the written form over the oral, introducing the practice of sending written messages to Congress rather than addressing the two houses in person as had formerly been the practice.

James Madison

Born in Port Conway, Virginia, in 1751, James Madison received a classical education under the tutorship of a Scotsman and his local parish minister. He attended the College of New Jersey (later Princeton), and after graduating in 1771, he returned to Virginia to study law.

Madison began his political career at the Virginia State Convention in Williamsburg in 1776, where he argued for freedom of religion at a time when Christian minorities were being persecuted in Virginia. In 1779 he was a member of the Continental Congress and was sent as a delegate to subsequent congresses. In 1783 he suggested that the congressional government institute an import duty in order to raise funds to pay off war debts, but he found his idea boycotted by most states. By 1786 when the Annapolis Convention met and decided to arrange a later meeting to discuss changes to the Articles of Confederation, Madison had become an important advocate for a strong, central government. He authored the Virginia Plan that Edmund Randolph presented at the 1787 Constitutional Convention in Philadelphia, and he also took notes on the proceedings at the convention that have served as an invaluable record for historians since the early nineteenth century.

From 1789 to 1797, he served in the House of Representatives, and was appointed secretary of state by Thomas Jefferson in 1801. In 1808 he was elected president. His presidency was a turbulent time, as the 1812 war broke out with England, and Madison and his cabinet were ignominiously forced to flee Washington, D.C., when British troops attacked the capital.

James Otis

James Otis was born in Barnstable, Massachusetts, in 1725. He studied literature and classics at Harvard, graduating in 1743. He continued his general education alone for two years before taking up the study of law, which he began to practice in 1748.

Otis rose to public prominence in 1761, when he resigned his prestigious position as the advocate-general for the British Crown and spoke out against the writs of assistance that empowered British customs officials to search citizens indiscriminately. Later that year he was elected to the Massachusetts legislature, in which capacity he attended the Stamp Act Congress in New York in 1765. Otis published several papers on the contemporary political situation: *A Vindication of the British Colonies* (1762), *The Rights of the British Colonies Asserted and Proved* (1764), and *Considerations on Behalf of the Colonists, in a Letter to a Noble Lord* (1765).

Tragically, in 1769 Otis was attacked in a Boston coffee shop by a disgruntled customs agent named John Robinson. Robinson severely injured Otis, inflicting on him serious brain damage that left Otis mentally impaired and unable to function in society. Otis spent his last years with his family on a farm in Andover, Massachusetts. It was there that he died during a thunderstorm in 1783, struck down by lightning while regaling his family with a story.

Pontiac

Pontiac was both a military leader and an inspiring orator. He stated that he was born along the banks of the Maumee River in Ohio in 1720, in the ancestral lands of the Ottawa tribe. When Pontiac became the chief of the Ottawa people, he began to firmly challenge British territorial claims in the area. In the early 1760s, he organized several neighboring tribes into a military association and launched a series of attacks on British outposts.

The attacks were mostly victorious; many British people—both soldiers and civilians—were killed, and several forts were destroyed. But the final challenge in this localized conflict was the attack of Fort Detroit, whose sturdy walls Pontiac was unable to breach. By July 1763 Pontiac and the commander at Fort Chartres agreed to make peace and suggested that both sides forget the horrors perpetrated and think of only the good.

In April 1769 Pontiac was killed by a Kaskasian Indian, who had ostensibly been bribed by a trader to assassinate the Ottawa chief.

Red Jacket

Red Jacket obtained his nickname from the red British army jacket that he became famous for wearing. He had been given the original garment by an officer during the American Revolution, at which time he fought with the British, and he was given subsequent versions of the same garment in later years. His real name, however, was Sagoyewatha, which means "He Who Keeps His People Awake." Unlike most of the great Native American orators, who were also known as great warriors, Red Jacket's fame is due solely to his oratorical skills, and he was actually accused of cowardice by several of his peers. He retorted, "A warrior? I am an orator! I was born an orator!"[3]

Red Jacket was an astute diplomat with an acute memory. On one famous occasion, he was arguing with Governor Daniel Tompkins of New York over the content of a treaty from several years earlier. Tompkins, certain that his assertion was correct, stated, "You have forgotten—we have it written down on paper." Red Jacket responded that the paper told a lie; he pointed to his forehead, saying, "I have it written down in here. . . . This is the book the Great Spirit gave us—it does not lie."[4] To Tompkins's embarrassment, the treaty in question was furnished, and Red Jacket was correct.

Born in 1750 near Seneca Lake, New York, Red Jacket spent most of his life defending the traditional religion and values of his people from the onslaught of European cultural colonialism. Nonetheless, several members of his own family embraced Christianity, and rifts developed within the Seneca people on the basis of these religious differences. Red Jacket also opposed the practice of removing Seneca children to American cities for education, arguing that they returned neither Native American nor white, with knowledge that was useless in the woods and false materialistic desires that could not be fulfilled. He also prophetically observed that integration into white cities held nothing but racist degradation for the Native American, saying that "if they [the Seneca] were raised among the white people, and learned to work, and to read as they do, it would only make their situations worse. They would be treated no better than negroes."[5]

Late in life, Red Jacket became an alcoholic, dying in 1830.

Tecumseh

Tecumseh was born near present-day Springfield, Ohio, around 1768, and he lived in the area of the Wabash River valley in Indiana. His mother was Creek and his father was Shawnee. He and his younger brother, Tenskwatawa (a mystical visionary known as "The Prophet") made it their mission to oppose further white expansion. They traveled extensively through the country making speeches and trying to create a union among the Wyandot, Delaware, Algonquia, Chippewa, Nanticoke, Creek, and Cherokee, believing that the Native American tribes must bond together to defend themselves against the whites. However, many leaders, such as the Creek chief Big Warrior, refused to support a confederation or war and failed to believe Tecumseh and Tenskwatawa's claim that they were divinely inspired. On one such occasion, Tecumseh rebuked Big Warrior for not wanting to fight, saying, "You do not believe that the Great Spirit has sent me. You shall know. I leave Tuckhabatchee directly, and shall go straight to Detroit. When I arrive there, I shall stamp on the ground with my foot and shake down every house in Tuckhabatchee."[6] By a strange coincidence, there immediately followed a disastrous earthquake that succeeded in fulfilling Tecumseh's threat.

Such incidents contributed to Tecumseh's success, and he and his brother established a village of their followers near the Wabash River called Prophet's Town. In addition to advocating unity, they promoted a return to traditional Native American values and sternly rejected white influences, especially alcohol.

After one of his long stints traveling, Tecumseh returned to Prophet's Town in 1811 to find it destroyed by Governor William Henry Harrison as part of his campaign against the Indians on the western frontier. In 1812, at the outset of the British-American war, Tecumseh joined the British forces for the second time (he had also aligned himself with them during the War of Independence) and was promoted to the rank of brigadier general in the British army. He was killed in 1813 while fighting alongside the British forces during the Battle of Thames near Ontario.

Joseph Warren

Joseph Warren was born in Roxbury, Massachusetts, in 1741. After graduating from Harvard College in 1759, Warren trained as a medical doctor and began practicing in the Boston area. From the time of the Stamp Act and the early political frictions centered around Boston, Warren was an eloquent voice of opposition to the British. In the 1760s he was a frequent contributor to the *Boston Gazette*, writing under the name of "A True Patriot," and continually renounced the tyrannical behavior of the British.

He gave two famous orations commemorating the Boston Massacre, one in March of 1772 and one in 1775. The first one is generally considered to be the better written and more substantial oration of the two. However, it was the later speech of 1775 that packed the hall with Bostonians, for British soldiers had warned beforehand that whoever dared to give the oration that year would not finish it alive—a challenge to which Warren rose eagerly.

Warren fought in the early battles of Concord and Lexington, where he was made a major general. Returning to Boston, he presided over the Provincial Congress, and when the Congress decided to take Bunker's Hill in June 1775, Warren rode into battle. The British won the battle, but as the American forces began to retreat, Warren was hit in the head by a musket ball and died.

George Washington

Washington was born in Virginia in 1732 and grew up there. After finishing school at age sixteen, he began working as a land surveyor in the western part of his native state. He expressed an interest in military life from an early age, and at nineteen he was appointed one of the adjutant generals of Virginia. In 1753, after his requests for the withdrawal of French troops from the western parts of Virginia were ignored, he led a successful mission that erected Fort Necessity and drove the French out of parts of Virginia. A couple years later he fought with General Edward Braddock at the disastrous Battle of Mononghela, during which Braddock and half his troops were killed. Although two horses were shot from under him, Washington managed to escape and return to Virginia, where he assumed command of the Virginian forces.

In 1754, at the age of twenty-two, he married the widow Martha Custis and then proceeded to pursue a quiet life as a planter. During this time he was elected as a delegate to the Virginia House of Burgesses, where he gained the reputation of being a wise and thoughtful person who was consistently moderate. He tracked the burgeoning discontent with British rule among his peers, and by the 1760s he firmly supported boycotting British goods and military resistance if necessary. As trouble brewed, especially in the North, Washington was sent to the First Continental Congress, and at the Second Congress he was unanimously elected commander in chief of the American forces. Not only did all who knew him have faith in his sound judgment and leadership abilities, but as a Virginian, he also represented Southern interests, counterbalancing the predominantly Northern forces based in Cambridge, Massachusetts, and making the engagement truly a continental one.

Leading a poorly outfitted and barely trained army from 1775 to 1783, Washington rallied the troops time and again, and his own fortitude in the face of hardship won him the adulation of America. At the war's end in 1783, Washington said a fond farewell to his troops and returned to his estate, where he dreamed of returning to a life of quietude in the Virginian hills. But this was not to be. His presence was still needed by the fledgling government, and he was asked to preside at the Constitutional Convention held in Philadelphia, where the new constitution creating a strong executive office was being written. After ratification Washington was elected as the nation's first president, an office he held from 1789 until 1796. Retiring from public office, he returned to Mount Vernon, where he died in 1799.

John Winthrop

John Winthrop, born in 1588, was the only child of an English country squire. He attended Cambridge University, was trained in law, and by his early twenties, he was married and established on his estate. But Winthrop's diaries reveal that much of his life was a struggle between resisting his attraction to carnal pleasures and aspiring to be as pure a Christian as he could. He thus came to believe that discipline is the essential element distinguishing humans from animals; hence, his preference for strict, oligarchical forms of government in which citizens are kept under tight control by their leader. For Winthrop, politics was a religious affair, and so he believed that as governor he had a God-given mandate to rule and, if necessary, to punish the people under his control.

Winthrop was a Puritan, part of a group of Protestants who believed that although the recently established Church of England had done much to shed the pomp and ceremony of the Catholic Church, too many Catholic practices still remained. The Puritans wished to "purify" the Church further, making possible a direct communication between the Christian and God, without the necessity for a clerical intermediary. However, members of the official religion of Anglicanism refused to allow the Puritans to practice, and immigration to the New World became an increasingly attractive option for them.

The wealthy and educated Winthrop was selected as governor of the newly chartered settlement that was to be established in Massachusetts. He rose to the challenge of the one-thousand-person migration with enthusiasm, excited at the thought of being the leader of a fledgling community of people whom he believed he could mold into his own vision. In a famous sermon that he gave as his ship approached America in 1630, Winthrop spoke of the settlement as being "a city upon a hill." He imagined that his settlement (what became Boston) would become a model example for those in England to follow.

On arrival, Winthrop's group fared considerably better than the earlier settlers in Virginia had, and within a few years, the population of Boston was growing steadily. In 1636, a mere six years after Winthrop's arrival, Harvard College was founded, and new towns and churches were planned and built every few years. However, Winthrop soon found his paternalistic style of governing challenged by the sense of freedom and independence that the settlers felt in their new country, where they were far removed from the stodginess and class rigidity of England. By the late seventeenth century more democratic forms of government had begun to replace Winthrop's Puritanical control, yet many of the fundamental precepts of the Puritans—their belief in hard work, in self-discipline, and in a tightly knit community—all survived as prominent features of American culture.

Notes

1. Quoted in William Jennings Bryan, ed., *The World's Famous Orations*, vol. 8: *America-I*. New York: Funk and Wagnalls, 1906, p. 22.

2. Quoted in Bryan, *The World's Famous Orations*, p. 63.

3. Quoted in W.C. Vanderwerth, ed., *Indian Oratory: Famous Speeches by Noted Indian Chieftains*. Norman: University of Oklahoma Press, 1971, p. 43.

4. Quoted in Vanderwerth, *Indian Oratory: Famous Speeches by Noted Indian Chieftains*, p. 43.

5. David J. Brewer, ed., *The World's Best Orations*. Chicago: Ferd. P. Kaiser, 1923, p. 425.

6. Quoted in Louis Thomas Jones, ed., *Aboriginal American Oratory: The Tradition of Eloquence Among the Indians of the United States*. Los Angeles: Southwest Museum, 1965, p. 85.

Chronology

1637
Pequot War: violence between the Pequot tribe and white settlers in the Boston area.

1676
King Philip's War: battles between Massachusetts settlers and the Algonquian tribes native to the area over issues of religious difference and white expansion.

1754
The Albany Conference is convened by the British to discuss the ongoing conflicts with the Native Americans and the French that have been occurring sporadically since the 1630s; the current postmaster general of the American colonies, Benjamin Franklin, proposes a plan for a union, but his idea is rejected.

1756
The ongoing fighting in North America between Britain and France merges with the Seven Years' War in Europe.

1758–1760
British forces take the main French forts at Louisberg, Ticonderoga, Niagara, and Duquesne (later Pittsburgh); this enables Britain to control the two important forks of the Ohio River; the British are also victorious at Quebec.

1763
The Treaty of Paris ends the Seven Years' War; France cedes Canada, the Mississippi, and control of India to Britain; the French keep some islands and fishing rights in North America, but their American empire is virtually destroyed; French Louisiana is ceded to Spain (France's ally during the war), which had lost Florida to the British; Britain declares the Appalachians the western limit of the colonies to preserve land to the west for Native Americans; nonetheless, American

colonists rapidly move west into the Ohio basin; Pontiac, of the Ottawa tribe, leads an uprising in an attempt to stay the western expansion; Britain decides to finance a British garrison in North America with American funds.

1764
The Sugar Act is passed, levying a tax on molasses imported to North America from territories other than British colonies, in an effort to finance the British military efforts.

1765
The Stamp Act is passed, with the ostensible reason of financing the defense of the colonies; by this law, tax stamps must be placed on newspapers, and legal and commercial documents; riots in Boston ensue; at the Stamp Act Congress in August, delegates meet to protest the Stamp Act.

1766
The Sugar Act tax is reduced, setting a precedent under which Americans have the power to change laws imposed by Britain; the Sons of Liberty is founded to propagate grassroots resistance; there are more riots in Boston against the Stamp Act; the Stamp Act is repealed in March in response to the protests of the American colonists; the Declaratory Act is passed, declaring Britain's right to bind the colonists in "all cases whatsoever."

1767
The Townshend Acts are passed, taxing lead, glass, tea, paper, and other items imported into the colonies; nonimportation and nonconsumption associations are revived in October to boycott the goods enumerated in the Townshend Acts; they appeal not only to the politicized urbanites but also to the rural population in their emphasis on the traditional values of self-sufficiency and self-reliance; British imports fall dramatically.

1768
The *Massachusetts Circular Letter* (Samuel Adams's letter denouncing the Townshend Acts) is sent to other provincial

assemblies, castigating the British and urging unity; in February, the Massachusetts governor condemns the letter and dissolves the Massachusetts legislature; John Hancock's sloop *Liberty* is seized in June, causing a mob to attack customs officials; four regiments of British troops arrive in Boston in October; British commissioner William Johnson negotiates the Treaty of Fort Stanwix with leaders of the Iroquois Confederation.

1769
The British and leaders of the southern Native American tribes sign the Treaty of Hard Labor Creek, which establishes a so-called permanent western boundary for land settlement.

1770
In March, five Bostonians die in violence between soldiers and a crowd in what later would become known as the Boston Massacre; the Townshend Tax is mostly repealed on March 5; nonimportation associations are dissolved, and imports rise 80 percent in the next three years.

1772
The Committees of Correspondence are established, and Boston becomes the center of the struggle against Britain; Rhode Island protesters burn *Gaspée*, a stranded British customs schooner; the British government establishes a Commission of Inquiry to find the perpetrators and send them to England for trial, thus suspending the criminal jurisdiction of the colony and angering the American colonists; however, the perpetrators are never found.

1773
The Tea Act taxes British teas imported into the colonies; the Boston Tea Party occurs—a cargo of East India tea is dumped into Boston's harbor in December by a group of dissidents organized by Samuel Adams.

1774
In response to the Boston Tea Party, Britain passes a series of laws against Boston and Massachusetts that the Americans

refer to as the Coercive or Intolerable Acts; these included the Boston Port Bill, which closed Boston's harbor and the Massachusetts Government Act, which annulled the colonial charter; delegates to the upper house would now be appointed by the king, rather than being elected; town meetings were practically forbidden; General Thomas Gage replaces Thomas Hutchinson as the governor of Massachusetts; the First Continental Congress is held in Philadelphia in September in response to the Boston port closing and the suspension of the Massachusetts government; this was the first intercolonial meeting since the 1765 Stamp Act Congress; a boycott of British manufactured goods is reinstituted, and in general, the delegates favor economic measures of persuasion rather than military ones; nonetheless, the Congress is considered an act of treason by the British; Patrick Henry, excited by the display of unity, famously declares: "I am not a Virginian, but an American"; the Declaration of Resolves is passed, articulating the rights of the Americans and denouncing the acts passed by the British Parliament as violations of these rights; condemnatory economic sanctions are imposed on the British in reprisal, and democratically chosen committees of local government are established.

1775

A weapons raid leads to the first battles of the war in April, as troops under General Gage meet colonists at Concord and Lexington; delegates from twelve of the colonies who had been indirectly elected by the Committees of Observation and Safety attend the Second Continental Congress in May; delegates decide to put the colonies in a state of defense, and George Washington is made the commander in chief of the American forces; battles occur at Breed's and Bunker Hills in June; both British and American losses are heavy; in August, Britain's King George officially declares that the colonies are in a state of rebellion.

1776

The Declaration of Independence is written by Thomas Jefferson and is signed by the eleven rebel colonies on July 4, 1776.

1777
The British take New York and Philadelphia but are defeated at Saratoga; at Valley Forge, Washington's winter camp, eleven thousand die during the long, hard winter.

1778
France joins America in the war, and Washington revives hope on this account.

1779
Spain joins the war.

1781
The British take Charlestown, but Cornwallis surrenders at Yorktown; the French navy wins supremacy at sea in October; the Articles of Confederation are ratified by the states.

1782
Peace negotiations with Britain begin; during a political crisis in England, Lord Frederick North falls and Lord Charles Rockingham briefly replaces him as prime minister.

1783
Treaty of Paris: Britain accepts the independence of the thirteen colonies, but it retains the West Indies and Canadian colonies; defeated British loyalists leave the victorious colonies and move to New Brunswick and Prince Edward Island.

1784
Treaty of Fort Stanwix: The new U.S. government signs a treaty with the Iroquois, which results in the Native Americans signing over more land for white settlement.

1785
Treaty of Hopewell: The United States concludes treaties with the Cherokee, Choctaw, and Chickasaw chiefs in which these tribes cede large tracts of land.

1786–1787
Shays's Rebellion: A group of farmers in western Massachu-

setts refuse to pay burdensome taxes and instigate an armed uprising.

1787

Constitutional Convention: Delegates meet to make revisions to the Articles of Confederation, and the result is the writing of a new constitution; the Northwest Ordinance establishes procedures for future land sales to settlers in the northwestern United States (between the Ohio and Mississippi Rivers) and outlines the organization of these areas into states once their populations reach that of the smallest state in the country.

1788

The U.S. Constitution is ratified; Washington is elected the first president.

1789

Washington is inaugurated; Hamilton heads the treasury; the French Revolution begins.

1790

The U.S. Supreme Court meets in New York.

1791

The Bill of Rights is ratified as the first ten amendments to the Constitution; U.S. forces are defeated by the Western Confederacy of Native American tribes (Miami, Shawnee, Delaware, Chippewa, Ottawa, Potawatomi) in present-day Ohio.

1793

George Washington's second term as president begins.

1794

At the Battle of Fallen Timbers, U.S. forces defeat the Western Confederacy tribes, thus destroying Native American control of the Ohio region; the Whiskey Rebellion occurs as western Virginian farmers refuse to pay taxes on whiskey.

1795

The Treaty of Greenville is signed between the Western Confederacy and the United States, by which the United States gains the right to settle the area between the Ohio and Mississippi Rivers (present-day Ohio), and Native American tribes gain recognition of their right to all of the remaining land not yet ceded.

1796
John Adams is elected president (1797–1801); Thomas Jefferson is elected vice president.

1798
The Alien and Sedition Acts are passed, restricting freedom of speech and freedom of the press by making criticism of the government illegal; the residence period necessary for immigrants to become citizens is lengthened.

1800
Thomas Jefferson is elected president (1801–1809).

1803
Jefferson purchases Louisiana from Napoléon.

1809
James Madison is elected president (1809–1817).

1811
Indian resistance is led by Tecumseh and "the Prophet"; at the Battle of Tippecanoe, Indiana's Governor William Henry Harrison defeats the Prophet and a mixed force of western tribes.

1814
At the Battle of Horseshoe Bend, General Andrew Jackson of Georgia penetrates the Creek fortress and defeats the Creek tribe.

1829
Jackson is elected president (1829–1837).

1830

In May, Congress passes the Indian Removal Act at President Jackson's behest; this legalizes the large-scale uprooting of hundreds of thousands of Native Americans in order to make way for white settlement.

1832

The Sauk chief Black Hawk attempts to reunify western tribes and reclaim Sauk lands east of the Mississippi, but he is captured by Jackson and renounces his attempts in the face of superior white power.

1833

Slavery is abolished in the British empire.

For Further Research

RALPH K. ANDRIST, *The American Heritage History of the Making of the Nation, 1783–1860.* New York: American Heritage, 1968.

BERNARD BAILYN, *The Ideological Origins of the American Revolution.* Cambridge, MA: Belknap Press of Harvard University, 1967.

DANIEL BOORSTIN, *The Americans: The Colonial Experience.* New York: Random House, 1964.

EDWARD COUNTRYMAN, *The American Revolution.* New York: Hill and Wang, 1985.

JOHN MACK FARRAGHER ET AL., *Out of Many: A History of the American People.* Englewood Cliffs, NJ: Prentice Hall, 1994.

JACK P. GREENE, ED., *The Reinterpretation of the American Revolution, 1763–1789.* New York: Harper and Row, 1968.

GERALD N. GROB AND GEORGE ATHAN BILLIAS, *Interpretations of American History: Patterns and Perspectives.* Vol. 1. New York: Free Press, 1982.

DICK HOWARD, *The Birth of American Political Thought, 1763–87.* Minneapolis: University of Minnesota Press, 1989.

PHILIP JENKINS, *A History of the United States.* New York: St. Martin's Press, 1997.

FRANCIS JENNINGS, *Empire of Fortune: Crowns, Colonies, and Tribes in the Seven Years' War in America.* New York: Norton, 1988.

MALDWYN A. JONES, *The Limits of Liberty: American History, 1607–1980.* Oxford, England: Oxford University Press, 1983.

ADRIENNE KOCH, *Power, Morals, and the Founding Fathers.* Ithaca, NY: Cornell University Press, 1961.

PAULINE MAIER, *From Resistance to Revolution: Colonial Radicals and the Development of American Opposition to Britain.* New York: Knopf, 1972.

DREW MCCOY, *The Elusive Republic: Political Economy in Jeffersonian America.* Chapel Hill: University of North Carolina Press, 1980.

MICHAEL MCGIFFERT, ED., *Puritanism and the American Experience.* Reading, MA: Addison-Wesley, 1969.

JOHN C. MILLER, *The Federalist Era, 1789–1801.* New York: Harper, 1960.

———, *The Origins of the American Revolution.* Boston: Little, Brown, 1957.

PERRY MILLER, *Errand into the Wilderness.* Cambridge, MA: Belknap Press of Harvard University, 1956.

S. MORGAN, *The Birth of the Republic.* Chicago: University of Chicago Press, 1977.

RODERICK A. NASH, *From These Beginnings: A Biographical Approach to American History.* New York: Harper and Row, 1973.

MARY BETH NORTON, *Liberty's Daughters: The Revolutionary Experience of American Women, 1750–1800.* Boston: Little, Brown, 1980.

RUSSELL B. NYE, *The Cultural Life of the New Nation.* New York: Harper, 1960.

RONALD F. REID, *American Rhetorical Discourse.* Prospect Heights, IL: Waveland Press, 1995.

JAMES RONDA, *Lewis and Clark Among the Indians.* Lincoln: University of Nebraska Press, 1984.

DEBORAH GILLIAN STRAUB, *Voices of Multicultural America: Notable Speeches Delivered by African, Asian, Hispanic, and Native Americans: 1790–1995*. New York: Gale Research, 1996.

RICHARD WHITE, *The Middle Ground: Indians, Empires, and Republics in the Great Lakes Region, 1650–1815*. New York: Cambridge University Press, 1991.

GORDON WOOD, *The Creation of the American Republic, 1776–1787*. Chapel Hill: University of North Carolina Press, 1998.

ALFRED F. YOUNG, ED., *The American Revolution: Explorations in American Radicalism*. De Kalb: Northern Illinois University Press, 1976.

Index

Adams, John, 16, 185
  and Declaration of Independence, 20
  legislation under, 33
Adams, Samuel, 104
  biographical information, 202–203
  and Boston Tea Party, 16
Algonquian Indians, 34, 35
  see also Native Americans
Alien and Sedition Acts (1798), 33
America
  as exemplar to the world, 194–95,
    196–97
  independence, 12–13
  as inspiring European revolutions,
    198–99
  international alliances of, 180–84
  settlements in, 17
  uniting with Great Britain, as
    impossible, 109–10
  unity in, 186–88
    advantages in, 174, 175–76
    advantages to, 177
    pride in, 174–75
    threats to, 176–77
  see also colonists; government; Native
    Americans
American Bible Society, 204
American Revolution
  causes of, 21–22
  celebrating anniversary of, 192–93
  first shot of, 19
  legacy of, 193–94
  and Native Americans, 35–36
Annapolis Convention (1786), 25
Anti-Federalists, 123
  vs. Federalists, 28–30
  political party of, 32
Arabella (ship), 79
aristocracy, 48
army. *See* standing army
Articles of Confederation
  amending, 25, 119
  problems with, 23–24
  writing, 22–23
  see also Constitution, U.S.

bank, national, 31–32
Bartholdi, Frederic, 200
Bill of Rights, 29–30
  see also Constitution, U.S.
Black Hawk (Sauk chief), 38, 167, 203
Boston Massacre (1770), 16, 46, 60–61
  British use of force in, vs. use of
    reason and liberty, 52–55
  horrors of, 51–52
  see also standing army
Boston Tea Party (1773), 16, 56, 202
Boucher, Jonathan, 93, 203–204
Boudinot, Elias, 191, 204
boycotts, 13, 15, 18, 56
Braddock, Edward, 146, 216
Bradley, Richard, 85
British Constitution, 48
British troops. *See* standing army
Bunker Hill, Battle of, 20, 104
Burke, Edmund, 66–67, 204–205
Burke, Thomas, 22
Burr, Aaron, 210

Cass, Lewis, 37–38
Channing, William, 115
checks and balances, 26, 134
Cherokee Indians, 36, 38
  see also Native Americans
Cherokee Nation v. Georgia, 38
Chicksaw Indians, 38
  see also Native Americans
Choctaw Indians, 38
  see also Native Americans
Coercive Acts (1774), 18, 57
colonists
  boycott on tea, 56
  British trade restrictions on, 41–42
  call to break free from Britain, 63–65,
    108–109, 110–13
  call for uniting, 62–63
  devotion to freedom and liberty by,
    69–71, 73
  educated in law, 71–72
  Great Britain as enslaving, 61–62
  limit of British power over, 72–73
  losing hope in Great Britain, 75–77